Italian Phrase Book

2500 Super Helpful Phrases and Words
You'll Want for Your Trip to Italy

Contents

Introduction

This is a short presentation of the Italian language. Thinking that you are supposed to learn as you go, you will find short bits of grammar and vocabulary here and there while taking a trip to Italy. Although, initially, you will find some basic information to help you through the rest of the book. In the First Section of the book, you will find an essential and easy description of how to read (Chapter 1), how to count and handle money (Chapter 2), how to talk about weather and time (Chapter 3), how to have a simple conversation with somebody you just met (Chapter 4), and how to ask questions politely (Chapter 5), in Italian.

In the Second Section, you will take a trip to Italy. This trip will give you the chance to learn new words while picking up pieces of grammar (grammar tips) on the way. You will first travel to Italy (Chapter 6), either by airplane or by other means of transportation, and then you will choose your favorite kind of accommodation and go around visiting museums, going shopping, and enjoying the Italian cuisine (Chapter 7). This trip will end with a linguistic overview of the Italian culture, delivered the way your grandparents would have delivered it: through old tales or proverbs and idioms (Chapter 8).

As anticipated, after the trip to Italy, you will find a section of Essential Grammar (Chapter 9). This is the grammar you need for the trip and a little bit more. At the end of the book, you will have the Essential Vocabulary (Chapter 10) that you found in this book, which will enable you to search both in Italian to English and in English to Italian.

Chapter 1 - Letters and Words

There is bad news and good news when you learn how to read in Italian. The bad news is that quite a few letters are pronounced differently from how you would pronounce them in English. The good news is that there are very few rules (five!) and they ALWAYS (with few exceptions) apply.

There are only five **vowels** in Italian:

A as in father

E as in bed

I as in pizza

O as in go

U as in rule

Vowels are always pronounced (never silent) and in the same way. Sometimes vowels appear one after the other, and you should always, at least, try to pronounce them all one after the other. This may be an entertaining challenge, like in *aiuole* (*flower beds*), the Italian word that carries all five vowels.

As for **consonants**, this is when the rules apply to **three** of them (c, g, h). The easy one is h, which is always silent, even in foreign words like *hotel* and *hamburger*. C and g are pronounced differently depending on what comes before or after them; they behave similarly when followed by vowels or h.

Five rules for reading:

1) C before vowels and h:

C is hard as in *cat* before a, o, u, and h:

casa (*house*), *cosa* (*thing*), *culla* (cradle), *chitarra* (guitar), *che* (which)

C sounds like *ch* in *chat* before i and e:

ciao (*hello/goodbye*), *cena* (*dinner*), *Cina* (*China*), *cioccolata* (*chocolate*), *ciuccio* (*pacifier*).

2) G before vowels and h:

G is hard as in *good* before a, o, u, and h:

gatto (*cat*), *gola* (*throat*), *gusto* (*flavor*), *ghetta* (*gaiter*), *ghiaccio* (*ice*)

G is pronounced like j in *jacket* before i and e:

giacca (*jacket*), *gioco* (*game*), *giusto* (*correct*), *gelato* (*ice cream*), *gita* (*trip*)

C and G sound different in three more cases:

3) C after S:

sc is hard as in *scout* before a, o, u, and h:

scatto (*click*), *scossa* (*shake,* [*electric*] *shock*), *scuola* (*school*), *schiaffo* (*slap*), *scherzo* (*joke*)

sc sounds like *sh* in *sheet* before i and e:

scialle (*shawl*), *scena* (*scene*), *sci* (*ski*), *sciocco* (*silly*), *sciupato* (*damaged*)

4) g before n:

gn like in **gnocchi** (*gnocchi*), **bagno** (*bathroom*), **sogno** (*dream*) sounds like the **gn** in *lasagna*

5) g before l:

gl like in *figlio* (*son*), *foglio* (*sheet*) sounds like **ll** in *million*

Otherwise, as you will see in the next section, consonants are usually pronounced as in English, with the exception of *r*, which is thrilled as in **bravò!**

The Alphabet

The Italian alphabet has only 26 letters, 5 vowels, and 21 consonants. The letters J, K, X, Y, and W only appear (more and more often nowadays) in foreign words.

A as in *father* (**padre**)

B as in *banana* (**banana**)

C as in *cat* (**gatto**) or *chocolate* (**cioccolato**)

D as in *dice* (**dado**)

E as in *bed* (**letto**)

F as in *flower* (**fiore**)

G as in *good* (**buono**) or *jacket* (**giacca**)

H **always silent**

I as in *pizza* (**pizza**)

L as in *letter* (**lettera**)

M as in *mother* (**madre**)

N as in *nonna* (**grandmother**)

O as in *opera* (**opera**)

P as in *peach* (**pesca**)

Q as in *queen* (**regina**)

R as in *bravo* (***bravò***)

S as in *sound* (***suono***)

T as in *turtle* (***tartaruga***)

U as in *rule* (***regola***)

V as in *valley* (***valle***)

Z as in *zone* (***zona***)

Expected and unexpected hiccups:

Doubles

As letters are (almost) always pronounced in the same way and each sound is (almost) always written in the same way, you can and must rely on what is written. Every letter matters, even when the same one is repeated like in the case of "*a double*": "***una doppia***". Few consonants can be doubled, and they are not pronounced twice; they are simply longer than usual. It matters as much as the difference between:

casa (*home*) and *cassa* (*register*), *caro* (*dear*) and *carro* (*wagon*), *polo* (*pole*) and *pollo* (*chicken*), *fato* (*fate*) and *fatto* (*done*), *ano* (*anus*) and *anno* (*year*), *nono* (*ninth*) and *nonno* (*grandfather*).

Word stress

You can get by without knowing where to stress a word, at the beginning, in the middle, at the end—everybody who makes an effort will understand you. As in English, you cannot tell where to stress a word from how it is written. But you can guess! Most Italian words are stressed on the second to last syllable: <u>ca</u>sa, ba<u>na</u>na.

This could be tricky for an English speaker since English long words are usually stressed on the first syllable (<u>sta</u>tion, <u>hos</u>pital, <u>res</u>taurant, etc.), and usually, their Italian counterparts are stressed on the penultimate (one before last) syllable: *sta<u>zio</u>ne*, *ospe<u>da</u>le*, *risto<u>ran</u>te*. This pattern is so frequent that Italians pronounce foreign words the same way and will say ***ham<u>bur</u>ger*** (with a silent h!).

You also can rely on one (and only) clue given by an accent on the last vowel for words that are stressed on the last syllable: *città* (*city*), *comò* (*chest of drawers*), etc., and it luckily distinguishes **papà** (*dad*) from **Papa** (*Pope*).

Chapter 2 - Numbers and Money

In this chapter, you will find the Italian number system and learn how to use cardinal and ordinal numbers. Cardinal numbers express amounts; ordinal numbers refer to an ordered sequence. Cardinal numbers refer to amounts; for example, when you need to say you need *five* (*cinque*) tickets for the train or you would like to buy *four* (*quattro*) apples or order *two* (*due*) glasses of wine. Ordinal numbers are further needed when you need to understand when to take a turn at the *second* (*seconda*) street, or that your seat is on the *third* (*terza*) row or your room is on the *fifth* (*quinto*) floor.

Cardinal numbers

Like in most languages, you need to memorize the first few numbers, and then it becomes easier to discover a system to be able to say any number.

When you pronounce the numbers' names, remember that there are only five **vowels** in Italian (A as in father, E as in bed, I as in pizza, O as in go, U as in rule) and you need to pronounce them all one after the other!

0 *zero*

1 *uno*

2 *due*

3 *tre*

4 *quattro*

5 *cinque*

6 *sei*

7 *sette*

8 *otto*

9 *nove*

10 *dieci*

11 *undici* (*un-* stands for *uno* and *-dici* for *dieci*)

12 *dodici*

13 *tredici*

14 *quattordici*

15 *quindici*

16 *sedici*

17 *diciassette*

18 *diciotto*

19 *diciannove*

After 19, you can easily put together the numbers once you know the tens, hundreds, and so on. As an example, here are the "twenties":

20 *venti*

21 *ventuno*

22 *ventidue*

23 *ventitré*

24 *ventiquattro*

25 *venticinque*

26 *ventisei*

27 *ventisette*

28 *ventotto*

29 *ventinove*

The tens:

10 *dieci*, 20 *venti*, 30 *trenta*, 40 *quaranta*, 50 *cinquanta*, 60 *sessanta*, 70 *settanta*, 80 *ottanta*, 90 *novanta*

The hundreds:

100 *cento*, 200 *duecento*, 300 *trecento*, 400 *quattrocento*, 500 *cinquecento*, 600 *seicento*, 700 *settecento*, 800 *ottocento*, 900 *novecento*

The thousands:

1000 *mille*, 2000 *duemila*, 3000 *tremila*, 4000 *quattromila*, 5000 *cinquemila*, 6000 *seimila*, 7000 *settemila*, 8000 *ottomila*, 9000 *novemila*

As you would have noticed, when there is only one thousand, the word is *mille,* but when there is more than one, the word is *mila.*

After the *thousands*, there are the *millions* (*un milione, due milioni, tre milioni...*) and the *billions* (*un miliardo, due miliardi...*).

Ordinal numbers

The first ten ordinal numbers are not systematic, but from the eleventh on, you may just drop the last vowel of the original number and attach -esimo: *undic-i* (*eleven*) becomes *undic-esimo* (*eleventh*).

Primo (*first*), *secondo* (*second*), *terzo* (*third*), *quarto* (*fourth*), *quinto* (*fifth*), *sesto* (*sixth*), *settimo* (*seventh*), *ottavo* (*eighth*), *nono* (*ninth*), *decimo* (*tenth*).

Undicesimo (*eleventh*), *dodicesimo* (*twelth*), *tredicesimo* (*thirteenth*), quattordicesimo (fourteenth), quindicesimo (fifteenth), sedicesimo (sixteenth), diciassettesimo (seventeenth), diciottesimo (eighteenth), diciannovesimo (nineteenth).

Ventesimo (*twentieth*), *ventunesimo* (*twenty-first*), *ventiduesimo* (*twenty-second*)...

trentesimo (*thirtieth*), *quarantesimo* (*forthieth*), *cinquantesimo* (*fiftieth*)... *centesimo* (*hundredth*), *milleimo* (*thousandth*).

GRAMMAR TIP – GENDER AND NUMBER in articles and ordinal numbers

Italian words end differently depending on whether they are feminine or masculine and singular or plural. Most of the time, the last vowel for the feminine singular is -a, feminine plural is -e, masculine singular is -o, masculine plural is -i.

Gender and number show in the articles:

la for *the* (feminine singular)

le for *the* (feminine plural)

una for *a* (feminine singular)

alcune for *some* (feminine plural)

il/lo, *the* singular (masculine singular)

i/gli, *the* plural (masculine plural)

uno/un for *a* (masculine singular)

alcuni for *some* (masculine plural)

When a determiner ending with a vowel (*la*, *le*, *una*, *lo*) is followed by a word beginning with a vowel, the determiner loses its vowel, and its loss is marked by an apostrophe: *la estate* becomes *l'estate* (*the summer*). The exception is for *uno*: the vowel disappears, but no apostrophe marks its place (*un amico*, *a friend* [masculine]).

Ordinal numbers follow this rule too:

Feminine:

La prima bambina (*the first girl*)

Le prime bambine (*the first girls*)

Masculine:

Il primo bambino (*the first boy*)

I primi bambini (*the first boys*)

Some singular masculine words end in -e and their plural counterpart ends in -i:

Mese (*month*) and *mesi* (*months*)

Money (*i soldi*)

Italy is in the Eurozone, and, like the other 19 of the 28 member states of the European Union, adopted the euro* (code: **EUR**) as its official *currency* (*valuta*). The Greek epsilon (€) and the first letter of the word Europe inspired the € symbol. The euro *banknotes* (*banconote*) are issued in €500, €200, €100, €50, €20, €10, €5. Each banknote (*banconota*) has its own color and is dedicated to an artistic period of European architecture. There are no *bills* (*banconote*) for 1 and 2 euros, but *coins* (*monete*). The euro is divided in 100 *cents* (*centesimi*) and coins are issued for 50c, 20c, 10c, 5c, 2c, and 1c.

*The word euro is written in the same way in Italian and English but it's pronounced quite differently! Remember every vowel is pronounced in the same way one after the other: 'e' as in *bed*, 'u' as in *rule*, 'r' as in *bravo,* and 'o' as in *go.*

Paying for something

Quant'è? for *how much is it?*

È costoso for *it is expensive*

È economico for *it is cheap*

Accettate carte di credito? for *do you accept credit card?*

Posso pagare con il bancomat? for *may I pay with my debit card?*

Posso pagare in dollari? For *may I pay with dollars?*

Certo, accettiamo carte di credito for *of course, we accept credit cards*

Prego, firmate la ricevuta for *please, sign the receipt*

Accettiamo solo contante for *we accept only cash*

Ho i traveller's cheque for *I have traveler's checks*

Posso farti un assegno? For *can I write you a check?*

Usually, *cash* (*i contanti*) is preferred over the *credit* (*carta di credito*) or *debit card* (*bancomat*). Also, when you buy anything in Italy, they are required by law to give you a *receipt* (*una ricevuta*).

GRAMMAR TIP: the conjugation of the verb *comprare* (to buy), *vendere* (to sell) and *pagare* (*to pay*)

Italian regular verbs conjugate for every person and tense: the form changes depending on who performs the action and when. There are three groups of regular verbs, and you can recognize them by the last three letters in their infinitive form. The first group ends in -are, like *comprare* (*to buy*) and *pagare* (*to pay*), the second group ends in –ere, like *vendere* and *spendere* (*to spend*), and the third group ends in –ire, like *partire* (*to leave*). When you conjugate a verb, it loses the infinitive ending (-are, -ere or -ire) and gains the end for a person in a particular time (present, past, future...). Usually, there are six different endings for six different persons: *io* (*I*), *tu* (*you*), *lei/lui* (*she/he*), *noi* (*we*), *voi* (*you* many) and *essi/loro* (*they*). Given that every person ends differently, in Italian, it is not important to mention the pronoun (*io, tu, lei, lui...*) and it can be simply dropped! When it comes to money, the verbs you may need most frequently are *vend-ere* (*to sell*), *compr-are* (*to buy*) and *pag-are* (*to pay*).

Present of **comprare** (*to buy*):

Io compro (i.e., compr-o) for *I buy*

Tu compri (i.e., compr-i) for *you buy*

Lei/lui compra (i.e., compr-a) for *s/he buys*

Noi compriamo (i.e., compr-iamo) for *we buy*

Voi comprate (i.e., compr-ate) for *you* (many) *buy*

Essi/Loro comprano (i.e., compr-ano) for *they buy*

Present of **vendere** (*to sell*):

Io vendo (i.e., vend-o) for *I sell*

Tu vendi (i.e., vend-i) for *you sell*

Lei/lui vende (i.e., vend-e) for *s/he sell*

Noi vendiamo (i.e., vend-iamo) for *we sell*

Voi vendete (i.e., vend-ete) for *you* (many) *sell*

Essi/loro vendono (i.e., vend-ono) for *they sell*

Present of **pagare** (*to pay*)

Io pago for *I pay*

Tu paghi for *you pay*

Lei/lui paga for *she/he pays*

Noi paghiamo for *we pay*

Voi pagate for *you (many) pay*

Essi/loro pagano for *they pay*

Other relevant verbs related to money are:

Chiedere in prestito for *to borrow*

Incassare un assegno for *to cash a check*

Costare for *to cost*

Girare un assegno for *to endorse*

Cambiare for *to change*

Prestare for *to lend*

Ordinare for *to order*

Dovere for *to owe*

Rimborsare for *to refund*

Risparmiare for *to save*

Spendere for *to spend*

Trasferire del denaro/dei soldi for *to transfer money*

At the bank (*in banca*) or the ATM

You can find an *ATM* (*il bancomat*) right outside or after the first door of a bank as well as at the airport or station. It is not common to find one in a store!

Dov'è il bancomat? For *where is the cash machine?*

ATMs usually allow you to choose your language, but there are keys on the board that may be in Italian only: **esatto** (*exact*), **conferma** (*confirm*), **esegui** (*enter*), **annulla/annullare** (*cancel*).

Dov'è la banca? For *where is the bank?*

Vorrei aprire un conto corrente for *I would like to open an account*

Vorrei fare un prelievo for *I would like to make a withdrawal*

Vorrei fare un versamento for *I would like to make a deposit*

Ho perso il mio bancomat for *I lost my debit card*

Ho perso la mia carta di credito for *I lost my credit card*

La mia carta non funziona for *my card does not work*

La mia carta è stata smagnetizzata for *my card has been deactivated*

La mia carta è stata rubata for *my card has been stolen*

La mia carta è stata trattenuta dal bancomat for *my card has been eaten by the ATM*

Il conto for *the account*

Il saldo for *the balance*

La banca for *the bank*

Il conto bancario for *the bank account*

La banconota/le banconote for *the bill or banknote*

I contanti for *cash*

Il cambio for *the exchange*

Il resto for *the change*

L'assegno/gli assegni for *the check*

Il conto for *the bill*

La carta/le carte di credito for *the credit card/cards*

Il cliente for *the client*

Il dollaro/i dollari for *the dollar/dollars*

Le spese for *the expenses*

L'interesse/gli interessi for *the interest/interests*

Il tasso d'interesse for *the interest rate*

Il prestito for *the loan*

Il vaglia postale for *the money order*

Il beneficiario/i beneficiari for *the payee/payees*

Il pagamento/i pagamenti for *the payment/payments*

La percentuale/le percentuali for *the percentage*

L'assegno personale for *the personal check*

Il prezzo/i prezzi for *the price/prices*

Il rimborso for *the refund*

Lo stipendio/gli stipendi for *the salary*

Le spese for *the spendings*

Il prelievo/i prelievi for *the withdrawal/withdrawals*

At currency exchange or exchange bureau (il cambiavalute)

You can change currency (*la valuta*) at most banks (*banche*), or you can find a currency exchange counter at the airport (*aeroporto*), station (*stazione*), and in some hotels (*alberghi*) and stores (*negozi*).

Beware that a currency exchange or bureau de change (*il cambiavalute*) is a business that makes its profit by buying foreign currency and then selling the same currency at a higher exchange rate. Sometimes you might want to ask whether they are charging you a *commission* or *fee* (*commissione*) or a *surcharge* (*un sovrapprezzo*) on the *purchase* (*acquisto*) or *sale* (*vendita*) of your money. Usually, the closer the buying and selling rates, the fairer the currency exchange.

Quant'è il cambio? For *how much is the exchange rate?*

Vorrei cambiare 100 dollari in euro for *I would like to change 100 dollars in euro*

Quant'è la commissione? For *how much is your fee/commission?*

Vorrei comprare/vendere degli euro for *I would like to buy/sell some euros*

Vorrei comprare/vendere dei dollari for *I would like to buy/sell some dollars*

Vorrei banconote di piccolo/grosso taglio for *I would like small/big bills*

Vorrei banconote di taglio misto for *I would like mixed bills*

Mi può cambiare queste banconote? for *could you break this in smaller bills?*

Chapter 3 - Time and Weather

In this chapter, we will use the number system to learn how to talk about time. In Italian, *time* and *weather* are expressed by the same word, *tempo*. Indeed, they are strictly connected as weather (*tempo*), and the temperature (*temperatura*) usually changes during the day (*giorno*), the months (*mesi*), the seasons (*stagioni*).

What time is it?

Times goes by in *ore* (*hours*), *minuti* (*minutes*), *secondi* (*seconds*), and a day (*giorno*) lasts 24 hours. It starts at *mezzanotte* (*midnight*), goes to *l'una* (1 a.m.), then *le due* (*2 a.m.*), then *le tre* (*3 a.m.*), and so on until **le ventitré e cinquantanove** (*23:59* or *11:59 p.m.*).

To ask and tell about time, you use the third person of *essere* (*to be*); the person will be either singular (*è* for *is*) or plural (*sono* for *are*) depending on the time. If it is one o'clock, then you will use the singular *è* (it is only one!); otherwise, you will use the plural *sono* (it is more than one!!).

Che ora è? or *Che ore sono?* for *what time it is?*

È l'una or *sono le due* for *it is 1 o'clock* or *it is two o'clock*

Sono le quattro e trenta minuti for *it is four-thirty*

Sono le diciassette e quarantacinque minuti e dieci secondi for *it is 5:45:10 p.m.*

Instead of the minutes, you can say what fraction of the hour it is: *un quarto* (*a quarter*), *mezza* (*a half*), *tre quarti* (*three quarters*). As in English, you use *e* (*and*) between the number and the portion of the hour:

Sono le undici e un quarto/ e mezza/ e tre quarti for *it is 11 and a quarter/and a half/and three quarters*

You can also say how many minutes to the hour:

Mancano dieci minuti alle quattordici for *ten to 2 p.m.*

Sono 5 all'una for *it is 5 to 1 a.m.*

Manca un quarto alle dieci for *it is a quarter to 10 a.m.*

In Italy, they use the 24-hour system, but you can use the 12-hour system and indicate which part of the day you are referring to:

la mattina for *the morning*

il pomeriggio for *the afternoon*

la sera for *the evening*

la notte for *the night*

Che ore sono?

Sono le due di notte for *it is two in the morning (a.m.)*

Sono le dieci del mattino for *it is 10 in the morning (a.m.)*

Sono le quattro del pomeriggio for *it is four in the afternoon (p.m.)*

Sono le 7 di sera for *it is 7 p.m.*

Sono le 11 della notte for *it is 11 p.m.*

GRAMMAR TIP: the use of *di* (*of*) with an article

The preposition *di* (*of*) indicates possession like *la casa di Matteo* (*the house of Matteo*). When followed by an article, they blend:

Di + *la* = *della* (*of the* – feminine singular)

Di + *le* = *delle* (*of the* – feminine plural)

Di + *il* = *del* or *di+lo*= *dello* (*of the* – masculine singular)

Di + *i* = *dei* or *di* + *gli* = *degli* (*of the* – masculine plural)

The days of the week

In Italian, the days of the week (*i giorni della settimana*) are not capitalized, they are all masculine but for Sunday, and they do not require a preposition in a sentence: *il lunedì* (*Monday*), *il martedì* (*Tuesday*), *il mercoledì* (*Wednesday*), *il giovedì* (*Thursday*), *il venerdì* (*Friday*), *il sabato* (*Saturday*), *la domenica* (*Sunday*).

Il lunedì vado in palestra, for *on Monday I go to the gym*

Vado a teatro sabato sera for *I go to the theater on Saturday evening*

To ask about the day of the week, you use *che giorno*, *what day*:

Che giorno è oggi? for *what day is today?*

Oggi è martedì. for *today is Tuesday*

What's the date?

In Italian, you use the ordinal number to refer to the first of any month and the cardinal number to refer to all the other days.

Il primo gennaio, but il *due/tre/quattro/cinque/... gennaio*

Usually, to say a date, you use *il* (*the*) followed by the number of the day like *primo, due, tre...* and by the preposition *di* (*of*) and the month:

Il primo di gennaio (January), *febbraio* (*February*), *marzo* (*March*), *aprile* (*April*), *maggio* (*May*), *giugno* (*June*), *luglio* (*July*), *agosto* (*August*), *settembre* (*September*), *ottobre* (*October*), *novembre* (*November*), *dicembre* (*December*).

To mention a date in the past, however, you may just say the number, the month, and the year: *il quattro novembre 1974*, *the fourth of November 1974*. To mention a year, though, in Italian, you say the whole number without breaking it into two parts.

1950 *millenovecentocinquanta* (*nineteen fifty*)

1999 *millenovecentonovantanove* (*nineteen ninety-nine*)

2020 *duemila e venti*

Il calendario delle feste

Italy has been a Catholic country for a long time and many holidays are Catholic, but not all!

The first holiday of the year is *the 1st of January* for **Capodanno** (literally the 'head of the year') or *primo dell'anno*. As part of the Catholic festivities, the sixth of January is *Epiphany* (**Epifania**), and sometime in the spring, two days celebrate *Easter* (**Pasqua**) and *Easter Monday* (**Lunedì dell'Angelo**).

After Easter, a series of non-religious national holidays follow and these are observed by most of the population as well. The 25th of April is the *Liberation Day* (**la Festa della Liberazione**) of Italy from the Nazi occupation in 1945. Italy celebrates *International Workers' Day* (**la festa dei lavoratori**) on the 1st of May, like in most countries, instead of Labour Day and people usually simply call it *il Primo Maggio*. June second is *Republic Day* (**la Festa della Repubblica**) to remember when, in 1964, Italy voted in favor of a Republic instead of a Monarchy.

In the summer, on August 15th Italians celebrate both the **Ferragosto** and the *Assumption* (**l'Assunzione**). The first was introduced by the emperor Augustus in 18 BCE as "Festivals

[Holidays] of the Emperor Augustus" to celebrate the harvest and the end of a long period of intense agricultural labor, and, over time, became a long weekend (*ponte di ferragosto*); the second is the bodily taking up of the Virgin Mary into Heaven at the end of her earthly life.

Then, in the Fall, is *All Saints' Day* (**Tutti i Santi** or **Ognissanti**) on November 1st, the *Immaculate Conception* (**l'Immacolata Concezione**) on December 8th and *Christmas Day* (**Natale**) and *Saint Stephen Day* (**Santo Stefano**) on December 25th and 26th respectively.

Surprisingly, for many travelers, is the extent to which a holiday impacts everything: transportation, stores, restaurants, and schools and students. So much that if you are planning to arrive on a major holiday, you may want to make sure there will be transportation to take you from the airport to your hotel, or how much the surcharge would be.

Che festa c'è il 6 gennaio? For *what holidays is on the 6th of January?*

Siete aperti per le feste? For *are you open during the holidays?*

Buone feste! for *Happy holidays!*

Buon Natale! for *Merry Christmas!*

Buon Capodanno! Or **Felice anno nuovo!** for *Happy New Year*

GRAMMAR TIP: the conjugation of the verb *celebrare* (*to celebrate*), present, past and future

You may like to use the verb **celebrare** (*to celebrate*) to refer to the holidays as well as all kinds of celebrations: birthdays, graduations, weddings, etc. As in English, you can always opt out and just use the verb **fare** (*to do*).

Come celebrerai le feste? For *how will you celebrate the holidays?*

Cosa fate per le feste? For *what are you doing for the holidays?*

Simple Present:

Io celebro for *I celebrate*

Tu celebri for *you celebrate*

Lei/lui celebra for *she/he celebrate*

Noi celebriamo for *we celebrate*

Voi celebrate for *you* (many) *celebrate*

Essi/loro celebrano for *they celebrate*

Present Perfect:

Io ho celebrato for *I celebrated*

Tu hai celebrato for *you celebrated*

Lei/lui ha celebrato for *she/he celebrated*

Noi abbiamo celebrato for *we celebrated*

Voi avete celebrato for *you* (many) *celebrated*

Essi/loro hanno celebrato for *they celebrated*

Future:

Io celebrerò for *I will celebrate*

Tu celebrerai for *you will celebrate*

Lei/lui celebrerà for *she/he will celebrate*

Noi celebreremo for *we will celebrate*

Voi celebrerete for *you* (many) *will celebrate*

Essi/loro celebreranno for *they will celebrate*

*In Italian, the present perfect is used (sometimes erroneously) more frequently as a past than a present perfect. And it happens that Italians would say *io ho fatto* when you say *I did*, and *io sono andato* when you say *I went*.

Speaking of time: how old are you?

To ask *how old are you?* you need to ask for how many years:

Quanti anni hai? for *how old are you?*

Io ho 5 anni for *I am 5 years old*

Quanti anni avevi nel 2001? for *how old were you in 2001?*

Quanti anni avrai l'anno prossimo? for *how old will you be next year?*

GRAMMAR TIP: the conjugation of avere

The verb *avere* (*to have*) is irregular, as in English and, as in English, is normally used to indicate possession or as an auxiliary for the past and conditional. In Italian, the two most frequent past tenses are the present perfect and the imperfect. You use the present perfect for actions completed (finished!) in the recent past and the imperfect for ongoing or habitual actions in the past: *mentre bevevo il caffè, ho finito i miei compiti* (*while I was drinking my coffee, I finished my homework*).

Simple Present:

Io ho* for *I have*

Tu hai* for *you have*

Lei/lui ha* for *she/he has*

Noi abbiamo for *we have*

Voi avete for *you have*

Loro/essi hanno* for *they have*

Present perfect:

Io ho avuto for *I had*

Tu hai avuto for *you had*

Lei/lui ha avuto for *she/he had*

Noi abbiamo avuto for *we had*

Voi avete avuto for *you* (many) *had*

Essi/loro hanno avuto for *they had*

Imperfect:

Io avevo for *I had*

Tu avevi for *you had*

Lei/lui aveva for *she/he had*

Noi avevamo for *we had*

Voi avevate for *you* (many) *had*

Essi/loro avevano for *they had*

Future:

Io avrò for *I will have*

Tu avrai for *you will have*

Lei/lui avrà for *she/he will have*

Noi avremo for *we will have*

Voi avrete for *you* (many) *will have*

Essi/loro avranno for *they will have*

*Remember the *h* is always silent

_____

_____

Essential vocabulary to speak and ask about time:

Quando? for *when?*

Ieri (*yesterday*), *oggi* (*today*), *domani* (*tomorrow*)

Quando arrivate in Italia? for *when do you arrive in Italy?*

Siamo arrivati ieri for *we arrived yesterday*

Arriviamo oggi for *we arrive today*

Arriveremo domani for *we will arrive tomorrow*

Che/Quale? for *which/on which?*

Che/quale giorno/giorni for *which day/days*

Che/quale settimana/settimane for *which week/weeks*

Che/quale mese/mesi for *which month/months*

Che/quale anno/anni for *which year/years*

In quale? for *in which?*

In quale secolo/secoli for *in which century/centuries*

In quale stagione? for *in which season?*

Prima/dopo for *before/after*

Presto/tardi for *early/late*

Mai/sempre for *never/always*

Piu tardi for *later*

A volte for *sometimes*

Qualche volta for *some times*

Una volta for *once*

Due volte for *twice*

Tre volte for *three times*

Più o meno for *more or less* (*sono più o meno le sei* for *it's six more or less*)

Circa for *about*

Weather (*tempo*) and climate (*il clima*)

Italian has one word, *tempo*, for both *time* and *weather*. Indeed, the weather does change in time with the *seasons*, *le stagioni* (singular: *la stagione*).

L'inverno, gli inverni for *the winter/winters*

La primavera, le primavere for *the spring/springs*

L'estate, le estati for *the summer/summers*

L'autunno, gli autunni for *the autumn/autumns*

When you ask and talk about the weather, you use either *essere* (*to be*) or *fare* (*to do*): apparently, the weather "does" itself.

L'inverno è freddo for *the winter is cold*

La primavera è fresca for *the spring is cool/crisp*

L'estate è calda for *the summer is hot*

L'autunno è piovoso for *the autumn is rainy*

Or

In inverno fa freddo for *in the winter is cold*

In estate fa caldo for *in the summer is hot*

To ask how the weather is, you always use *fare* (*to do*), but to answer, you can use either *fare* or *essere*:

Che tempo fa? for *how is the weather?*

Fa bello/brutto for *the weather is good/bad*

È bello/brutto for *the weather is good/bad*

Weather and temperature

Italy uses the metric system and temperatures are expressed in *Celsius scale* (*Scala Celsius*), which is divided into *centigrade degrees* (*gradi centigradi*). With this system, water freezes at *zero* °C (*zero*) and boils at *cento* °C (*100*). Temperatures range between - 10 °C (14 °F), to 0 (32 °F) and 10 °C (50 °F) during winter and between 20 °C (68 °F) and 40°C (104°F) during the summer.

Another difference is that, in English, the temperature *is*, while in Italian, *ci sono* (*there are*) degrees of temperature:

Qual è la temperatura oggi? For *what's the temperature today?*

Quanti gradi ci sono fuori? For *what's the temperature* (literally: how many degrees there are) *outside?*

Ci sono 21 (ventuno) gradi celsius (circa 70 gradi Fahrenheit) for *it's 21 degrees celsius (about 70 Fahrenheit)*

Essential vocabulary to talk about the weather

Bel tempo for *it's good weather*

Brutto tempo for *it's bad weather*

Il cielo for *the sky*

Il sole *for the sun*

La brina for *the frost*

La pioggia for *the rain*

La grandine for *the hail*

Il temporale for *the storm*

La neve for *the snow*

Il ghiaccio for *the ice*

La nebbia for *the fog*

La foschia for *the haze/mist*

Il lampo for *lightning*

La rugiada for *the dew*

Il vento for *the wind*

L'arcobaleno for *the rainbow*

Il sole for *sun*

La nuvola/le nuvole for *cloud/clouds*

Piove for *it's raining*

Diluvia for *it's pouring*

Grandina for *it's hailing*

Nevica for *it's snowing*

È umido for *it's humid*

È nuvoloso for *it's overcast*

C'è il sole for *it's sunny*

C'è il vento for it's windy

C'è la nebbia for it's foggy

C'è la pioggia for it's rainy

C'è burrasca for *it's stormy*

Ci sono lampi e tuoni for *lightning and thunder*

Piove a catinelle for *it rains cats and dogs*

GRAMMAR TIP: the use and conjugation of fare (to do)

Io faccio for *I do*

Tu fai for *you do*

Lei/lui fa for *she/he does*

Noi facciamo for *we do*

Voi fate for *you* (more than one) *do*

Loro/essi fanno for *they do*

Fare is a very useful word, especially in fixed expressions that might be tricky for an English speaker:

Fare il biglietto for *to buy a ticket*

Fare un viaggio/una gita for *to take a trip/an excursion*

Fare una passeggiata for *to take a walk*

Fare la fila for *to wait in line*

Fare una fotografia for *to take a picture*

Fare finta for *to pretend*

Far vedere for *to show*

Fare tardi for *to be late*

Fare presto for *to be quick*

Fare alla romana for *to go Dutch*

Fare la spesa for *do the shopping*

Fare le spese for *to go shopping*

Fare il pieno for *to fill up the gas tank*

Fare colazione for *to have breakfast*

Fare la doccia for *to have a shower*

Chapter 4 - Greetings, Salutations, and Introductions

Now you can read and use very frequent common phrases and learn how to meet with people.

Greetings, pleasantries, and salutations

Salve for *hello*

Buon giorno for *good morning*

Buon pomeriggio for *good afternoon*

Buona sera for *good evening*

Buona notte for *goodnight*

Arrivederci for *so long*

A presto for *see you soon*

A domani for *until tomorrow*

Ciao for *hello* and *goodbye*

Grazie for *thank you*

Prego for *you are welcome*

Benvenuto for *welcome*

Signorina for *signorina*

Signora for *Mrs*

Signore for *Mr*

Signori for *Mr and Mrs*

Introductions and basic conversation

For a basic conversation, you need three verbs: *chiamarsi* (*to be named, to be called*), *essere* (*to be*) and *stare* (*to be, to stay*).

When introducing yourself or somebody else, you use the verb *chiamarsi* (literally: *to call oneself*).

_____

_____

GRAMMAR TIP: how to conjugate a verb

In Italian, verbs change their ending depending on the person (who performs the action). There are six persons: *io* (*I*), *tu* (*you*), *lei/lui* (*she/he*), *noi* (*we*), *voi* (*you* – more than one) and *loro/essi* (*they*). *Chiamarsi* is a very particular verb, and when you use it, it divides itself into *chiamare* (*to call*) and *-si* (*oneself*) and both change depending on the person:

Io mi chiamo means *my name is* (literally: *I call myself*

Tu ti chiami for *your name is* (literally: *you call yourself*)

Lei/lui si chiama for *her/his name is* (literally: *she/he calls herself/himself*)

Noi ci chiamiamo for *our names are* (literally: *we call ourselves*)

Voi vi chiamate for *your names are* (literally: *you call yourselves*)

Loro/essi si chiamano for *their names are* (literally: *you call yourselves*)

Mi chiamo Lara for *my name is Lara*

Lei come si chiama? for *what is your name?* (formal)

Tu come ti chiami? for what is your name? (informal)

You can alternatively use the verb *to be* (*essere*) for introductions:

Buon giorno, noi siamo la signora e il signor White. Voi come vi chiamate?

Good morning, we are Mrs. and Mr. White. What's your name? (formal)

Noi siamo Marco e Maria, i cugini di Francesco.

We are Marco and Maria, Francesco's cousins.

GRAMMAR TIP: the conjugation of *essere* (*to be*), present, past and future

This verb, like in English, is highly irregular and most needed:

Present:

Io sono for *I am*

Tu sei for *you are*

Lui/lei è for *she/he is*

Noi siamo for *we are*

Voi siete for *you (more than one) are*

Essi/loro sono for *they are*

Past:*

Io sono stato for *I was*

Tu sei stato for *you were*

Lei è stata/lui è stato for *she/he was*

Noi siamo stati for *we were*

Voi siete stati for *you* (many) *were*

Essi/loro sono stati for *they were*

Future:

Io sarò for *I will be*

Tu sarai for *you will be*

Lei/lui sarà for *she/he will be*

Noi saremo for *we will be*

Voi sarete for *you* (many) *will be*

Essi saranno for *they will be*

* the past is rendered with the most frequently used past tense rather than correctly translated with the less frequently used preterit *(io fui, tu fosti, lei/lui fu, noi fummo, voi foste, essi furono)*, especially in the north of Italy.

Sometimes *families* (*famiglie*) gather together and you may need to introduce yours or understand the relationship between whoever is being introduced to you:

Buongiorno, io sono Marco, questa è mia moglie, Marcella, e questi sono i nostri figli, Pietro e Luca.

Good morning, I am Marco, this is my wife, Marcella and these are our sons, Pietro and Luca.

Famiglia (la famiglia, le famiglie) for *family, families*

Moglie (la moglie, le mogli) for *wife, wives*

Marito (il marito, i mariti) for *husband, husbands*

Madre (la madre, le madri) for *mother, mothers*

Padre (il padre, i padri) for *father, fathers*

Figlio (il figlio, i figli) for *son, sons*

Figlia (la figlia, le figlie) for *daughter, daughters*

Fratello (il fratello, i fratelli) for *brother, brothers*

Sorella (la sorella, le sorelle) for *sister, sisters*

Zia (la zia, le zie) for *aunt, aunts*

Zio (lo zio, gli zii) for *uncle, uncles*

Cugina (la cugina, le cugine) for *cousin, cousins (feminine)*

Cugino (il cugino, i cugini) for *cousin, cousins (masculine)*

Nipote (il nipote, i nipoti) for *nephew, nephews and grandson, grandsons*

Nipote (la nipote, le nipoti) for *niece, nieces and granddaughter, granddaughters*

Nonna (la nonna, le nonne) for *grandmother, grandmothers*

Nonno (il nonno, i nonni) for *grandfather, grandfathers*

Suocera (la suocera, le suocere) for *mother-in-law, mother-in-laws*

Suocero (il suocero, i suoceri) for *father-in-law, father-in-laws*

Nuora (la nuora, le nuore) for *daughter-in-law, daughter-in-laws*

Genero (il genero, i generi) for *son-in-law, son-in-laws*

These are the common replies when being introduced or answering to an introduction:

Piacere di conoscerti/conoscerla for *pleased to meet you (informal/formal)*

Molto piacere for *very pleased [to meet you]*

Piacere for *pleased [to meet you]*

As in English, during introductions, you can reply asking how they are, and to do so, you use *stare* (literally *to stay*):

Come stai/sta? for *how are you?* (informal/formal)

Io sto bene e tu? for *I am well and you?*

Noi stiamo bene e voi? for *we are well and you?*

Bene grazie e tu/lei? for *well, thank you, and you?* (informal/formal)

Or you may want to say *molto bene* (*very well*), *meglio* (*better*) *non c'è male* (*not bad*), *così così* (*so and so*), *non bene* (*not well*), *male* (*badly*).

If you want to say more about how you are, you may need to use *essere*: *sono riposato/stanco* (I am rested/tired), *sono malato/guarito* (I am sick/healed), *sono raffreddato* (*I have a cold*)...

GRAMMAR TIP: the conjugation of *stare* (*to be, to stay*)

Io sto bene for *I am well*

Tu stai bene for *you are well*

Lui/lei sta bene for *she/he is well*

Noi stiamo bene for *we are well*

Voi state bene for *you (many) are well*

Essi/loro stanno bene for *they are well*

Stare is also used in a series of very frequent fixed expressions:

Stare zitta for *to be quiet*

Stare attento for *to pay attention*

Stare con qualcuno for *to be in a relationship with*

Stare fermo for *to keep still*

Stare fuori for *to be outside*

Stare a pennello for *to fit like a glove*

Stare in guardia for *to be on one's guard*

Stare in piedi for *to be standing*

As in English, you can also ask *how is it going* saying:

Come va? for *how is it going?* or *how are you?*

Va bene/benissimo for *it is going well/very well* or *I am well/very well*

Va tutto bene for *all is going well*

Grazie for *thank you*

Prego for *you're welcome*

Per favore for *please*

Certo for *sure/of course*

Dica for *please, tell me*

Non parlo italiano [molto bene] for *I do not speak Italian [very well]*

Per favore, potrebbe parlare lentamente? for *could you, please, speak slowly?*

Può ripetere, per favore? for *could you repeat, please?*

Non capisco for *I do not understand**

Capisco for *I understand*

Cosa significa? for *what does that mean?*

Come si dice/si chiama questo in italiano? for *how do you say this in Italian?*

Potrebbe scrivermelo? for *could you please write this down for me?*

Parli inglese? For *do you speak English?*

C'è qualcuno che parla inglese? For *does anybody speak English?*

Per favore, potrebbe parlare inglese? For *could you please speak English?*

*To make a negative sentence in Italian, you only need to place the word *non* (*not*) before the verb.

GRAMMAR TIP: the conjugation of *parlare* (*to speak*), *scrivere* (*to write*), *ripetere* (*to repeat*), *capire* (*to understand*)

Simple Present of *parlare* (*to speak*):

Io parlo for *I speak*

Tu parli for *you speak*

Lei/lui parla for *she/he speaks*

Noi parliamo for *we speak*

Voi parlate for *you* (many) *speak*

Essi/loro parlano for *they speak*

Simple Present of *scrivere* (*to write*):

Io scrivo for *I write*

Tu scrivi for *you write*

Lei/lui scrive for *she/he writes*

Noi scriviamo for *we write*

Voi scrivete for *you* (many) *write*

Essi/loro scrivono for *they write*

Simple Present of *ripetere* (*to repeat*):

Io ripeto for *I repeat*

Tu ripeti for *you repeat*

Lei/lui ripete for *she/he repeats*

Noi ripetiamo for *we repeat*

Voi ripetete for *you* (many) *repeat*

Essi/loro ripetono for *they repeat*

Simple Present of *capire* (*to understand*):

Io capisco for *I understand*

Tu capisci for *you understand*

Lei/lui capisce for *she/he understand*

Noi capiamo for *we understand*

Voi capite for *you* (many) *understand*

Essi/loro capiscono for *they understand*

GRAMMAR TIP: *can* (*posso*) **and** *could* (*potrei*)

When you ask for something, as in English, in Italian, you can either use *posso?* (*can I?*) or *potrei?* (*could I?*) depending on the circumstances and how polite you would like to be. As in English, they are both followed by the infinitive form of a verb: *posso ripetere* (*I can repeat*) or *potrei ripetere* (*I could repeat*), *puoi ripetere* (*can you repeat?*) or *potresti ripetere* (*could you repeat?*).

Simple Present:

Io posso for *I can*

Tu puoi for *you can*

Lei/lui può for *she/he can*

Noi possiamo for *we can*

Voi potete for *you* (many) *can*

Essi/loro possono for *they can*

Present conditional:

Io potrei for *I could*

Tu potresti for *you could*

Lei/lui potrebbe for *she/he could*

Noi potremmo for *we could*

Voi potreste for *you* (many) *could*

Essi/loro potrebbero for *they could*

Present perfect:

Io ho potuto for *I could (in the past)*

Tu hai potuto for *you could*

Lei/lui ha potuto for *she/he could*

Noi abbiamo potuto for *we could*

Voi avevte potuto for *you* (many) *could*

Essi/loro hanno potuto for *they could*

Present perfect conditional:

Io avrei potuto for *I could have*

Tu avresti potuto for *you could have*

Lei/lui avrebbe potuto for *she/he could have*

Noi avremmo potuto for *we could have*

Voi avreste potuto for *you* (many) *could have*

Essi/loro avrebbero potuto for *they could have*

Future:

Io potrò for *I will be able to*

Tu potrai for *you will be able to*

Lei/lui potrà for *she/he will be able to*

Noi potremo for *we will be able to*

Voi potrete for *you* (many) *will be able to*

Essi/loro potranno for *they will be able to*

Chapter 5 - Asking Questions

In this chapter, you will find what words better translate the English question words in different situations. And you will learn how to ask questions politely and give (unfortunately) negative answers.

GRAMMAR TIP: the conditional is polite!

To ask for something politely, when ordering at a restaurant, on the plane, buying tickets, asking for directions, in Italian, you use the conditional of *volere* (*to want*), which corresponds to using *would*, but often translates as *would like*:

Present Indicative:

Io voglio for *I want*

Tu vuoi for *you want*

Lei/lui vuole for *she/he wants*

Noi vogliamo for *we want*

Voi volete for *you* (many) *want*

Essi/loro vogliono for *they want*

Present Conditional:

Io vorrei for *I would*

Tu vorresti for *you would*

Lei/lui vorrebbe for *she/he would*

Noi vorremmo for *we would*

Voi vorreste for *you would*

Essi/loro vorrebbero for *they would*

GRAMMAR TIP: the conjugation of *scusarsi* **(***to apologize***)**

As in English, another way to be polite is to excuse yourself. *Scusarsi* is a reflexive verb like *chiamarsi* (*to be named*) and has two parts: the infinitive *scusarsi* breaks into the verb stem (*scus-*) and the reflexive pronoun (*-si*). Both change for each person! The pronoun is placed in front of the verb, which is conjugated like a regular verb ending in -are (as if it was *scusare*, which means *to excuse*). Basically, *scusarsi* (*to apologize*) in Italian, matches *to excuse oneself.*

Simple present:

Io mi scuso for *I apologize*

Tu ti scusi for *you apologize*

Lei/lui si scusa for *she/he apologizes*

Noi ci scusiamo for *we apologize*

Voi vi scusate for *you* (many) *apologize*

Essi/loro si scusano for *they apologize*

Mi scusi, sa dirmi dove, quando, perché...?

Excuse me, can you tell me where, when, why...?

_____

_____

What

44

There are three different ways to ask *what*: *che, cosa,* and *che cosa.* When it is possible to substitute *what* with *which,* you can use *che*; otherwise, you use either *che cosa* or *cosa.*

Che giorno è oggi? for *what day is today?*

Che ora è? for *what time is it?*

Che cosa/cosa c'è da mangiare al ristorante? for *what is there to eat at the restaurant?*

Che cosa/Cosa fanno nel pomeriggio? for *what do they do in the afternoon?*

Cos'è questo/quello? for *what is this/that?*

Cosa vorresti fare? for *what would you like to do?*

Who

The word *chi* corresponds to the word *who*:

Chi sei? for *who are you?*

Chi sono questi bambini? for *who are these children?*

Chi è la ragazza con Paolo? for *who is the girl with Paolo?*

Where

You use *dove* for *where*:

Dove sono i nostri posti? for *where are our seats?*

Dov'è il teatro/la stazione/il ristorante...? for *where is the theater/the station/the restaurant?*

How?

Come is used to translate *how* and is used with *essere* to find out how people or things are:

Com'è la pizza? for *how is the pizza?*

Com'è la vacanza? for *how is the vacation?*

Come sono le spiagge? for *how are the beaches?*

Come stai? for *how are you?*

Come sta? for *how is she/he?*

Come stanno i tuoi genitori? for *how are your parents?*

As you saw in Chapter 2, *come* (*how*) with *chiamarsi* (*be named, be called*) is used to ask somebody's name: *come ti chiami?* for *what's your name?* and *mi chiamo Mario* for *my name is Mario*

Why?

Perché is used for both *why* and *because*:

Perché ridi for *why are you laughing?*

Perché andate in Italia for *why are you going to Italy?*

Perché suoni la chitarra for *why do you play the guitar?*

Perché è divertente for *because it is funny*

Perché i nostri genitori vivono in Italia for *because our parents live in Italy*

Perché mi piace for *because I like it*

When

Quando is used for *when*:

Quand'è il concerto? for *when is the concert?*

Quando parte il treno? for *when does the train leave?*

How much and how many

Quanto is used for *how much,* refers to a quantity, and varies with gender:

Quanto costa? for *how much does it cost?*

Quant'è? for *how much is it?*

Quant'è il vestito/il biglietto/il cambio? for *how much is the dress/the ticket/the exchange rate?*

Quanto pesa? for *how much does it weigh?*

Quanto dura? for *how long does it last?*

Quanto denaro hai? for *how much money do you have?*

Quanta pizza vuoi? for *how much pizza would you like?*

Quanti is used for *how many* and it varies with gender too:

Quante figlie avete? for *how many daughters do you have?*

Quanti figli avete? for *how many sons do you have?*

Which

Which is either ***quale*** for *which one* or ***quali*** for *which ones* and both can be replaced by ***che***:

Quale giorno parti? for *on which day do you leave?*

Quale pizza vuoi? for *which pizza do you want?*

Quale è la capitale d'Italia? for *which [city] is the capital of Italy?*

Quali mesi sono freddi? for *which months are cold?*

Quali gusti ti piacciono? for *which flavors do you like?*

Che giorno parti? for *on which day do you leave?*

Che pizza vuoi? for *which pizza do you want?*

Che gusti ti piacciono? for *which flavors do you like?*

Is there / are there?

Often in English, *is there? are there?* are used to ask for something that you are looking for, like a restaurant, bathroom, or taxi. The words ***c'è*** and ***ci sono*** correspond to the English *there is* and *there are* respectively. These words are used in the same order to both state there is something there and to ask: is there something? A rising tone for the question makes the difference:

C'è un ristorante vicino all'albergo for *there is a restaurant close to the hotel*

Ci sono dei negozi vicino alla stazione for *there are some stores nearby the station*

C'è un ristorante vicino al teatro? for *is there a restaurant close to the theater?*

Ci sono dei negozi vicino al museo? for *are there some stores nearby the museum?*

Ecco

The word *ecco* matches the English *here is* and *here are* (also *there is* and *there are*) and might be a likely answer to an *is there/are there* question:

Ci sono ancora due biglietti per il film? for *are there still two tickets for the movie?*

Ecco i biglietti for *here are the tickets*

C'è ancora un tavolo per quattro? for *is there still a table for four?*

Ecco il vostro tavolo for *here is your table*

Ecco il ristorante! for *here is the restaurant!*

Ecco il giornale! for *here is the newspaper!*

Ecco i calzini! for *here are the socks!*

Eccomi for *here I am*

Eccoti for *here you are*

Eccola for *here she is*

Eccolo for *here he is*

Eccoci for *here we are*

Eccovi for *here you (many) are*

Eccoli for *here they are*

GRAMMAR TIP: Negative sentences

To make a negative sentence in Italian, you only need to place the word *non* (*not*) before the verb:

Non c'è acqua nel bagno for *there is no water in the bathroom*

Non ci sono asciugamani nel bagno for *there aren't any towels in the bathroom*

Non ci sono elefanti allo zoo? for *aren't there elephants at the zoo?*

Mi scusi, c'è un bagno? for *excuse me, is there a bathroom?*

No, non c'è for *no, there is not*

Ci sono ancora dei biglietti per il concerto? for *are there still tickets for the concert?*

No, non ce ne sono più for *no, there aren't any more*

This is true for any kind of sentence:

Non c'è il sole for *it is not sunny*

Non piove for *it is not raining*

_____

_____

Chapter 6 - Traveling

Imagine that you are on your first trip to Italy, and pick up as many words and grammar as you can on your way there. Most people use an *airplane* (*aeroplano*) *to fly* (*volare*) there in as little time as possible. Otherwise, to get there or travel around Italy, you may end up using different *forms of transportation* (*mezzi di trasporto*), like *trains* (*treni*), *busses* (*autobus*), *ferries* (*traghetti*) or *rental cars* (*macchine a noleggio*). Last, but not least, you will probably go around a lot during your visit on *foot* (*a piedi*) and by *public transportation* (*trasporto pubblico*), like busses, *taxis* (*taxi*) and *steamboats* (*vaporetti*)—if you travel to Venezia.

Flying

On the plane

When you step on the plane on your way to Italy, you will show your *boarding pass* (*carta d'imbarco*) to *the flight attendant* (*l'assistente di volo*). She or he will point you to your *seat* (*il sedile, il posto*) or your *seats* (*i sedili, i posti*). Once you found your seat, you may need to first find some room for your *carry-on* (*il bagaglio a mano*).

Dove posso sistemare il mio bagaglio a mano?

Where could I put my carry-on?

Usually, you should put your carry-on in the *overhead compartment* (***nella cappelliera***) and your personal belongings, whether it is your purse (***borsetta***) or messenger bag (***borsa a tracolla***), *under the seat in front of you* (***sotto al sedile di fronte***). Sometimes, this may be more challenging than foreseen and you might need to ask:

Mi scusi mi può aiutare a sistemare il mio bagaglio?

Excuse me, could you help me with my luggage?

When everyone is all aboard and in their assigned seats, *the pilot* (***il pilota***) will give her/his greetings and announcements and the flight attendants (***gli assistenti di volo***) will participate in the (nowadays media delivered) *instructions in case of emergencies* (***istruzioni in caso di emergenza***) and make sure you know where the *emergency exits* (***uscite di emergenza***) and the *life-vests* (***giubbotti di salvataggio***) are.

Getting ready:

As soon as all passengers are on board (sometimes earlier), they will be advised to take their *seats* (***posti a sedere***) and fasten *their seatbelts* (***le loro cinture di sicurezza***). To prepare for *the take off* (***il decollo***), they will also be asked *to turn their electronics off* (***spegnere i dispositivi elettronici***), close the seat *table* (***tavolo***) in front of them, and put their *seat back* (***schienale***).

The *take off* (***il decollo***):

Quando decolliamo? for *when do we take off?*

Quando decolleremo? for *when will we take off?*

Quando siamo decollati? for *when did we take off?*

Siamo decollati alle 9 e 30 for *we took off at 9:30*

Siamo decollati con mezz'ora di ritardo for *we took off half an hour late*

Siamo decollati in anticipo for *we took off early*

Ho paura di volare for *I am afraid to fly*

While flying:

There are so many questions you may need to ask or things you need to say during your flight. In case you would like to start practicing, here are a few:

Cabina for *cabin*

Il vassoio for *the tray*

Potrei avere un bicchier d'acqua? for *may I have a glass of water?*

Vorrei una spremuta d'arancia for *I would like an orange juice*

Potrei avere qualcosa da mangiare? for *may I have something to eat?*

Quando verrà servita la cena/il pranzo/la colazione? for *when will dinner/lunch/breakfast be served?*

Cosa c'è per cena/pranzo/colazione? for *what are the options for dinner/lunch/breakfast?*

Io (non) ho un pasto speciale for *I (don't) have a special meal*

Ho ordinato un pasto per bambini/ragazzi for *I ordered a meal for children (0-24months/2-12years old)*

Ho ordinato un pasto... for *I ordered a... meal*

Vegetariano asiatico for *asian vegetarian*

Kosher for *kosher*

Musulmano for *muslim*

Indù for *hindu*

Leggero for *bland*

Senza glutine for *gluten free*

Ipocalorico for *low calories*

Ipocolesterolemico or **a basso contenuto di colesterolo** for *low cholesterol*

Iposodico for *low salt*

Senza lattosio for *lactose free*

A base di pesce for *fish*

Vegano for *vegan*

Vegetariano for *vegetarian*

Dov'è il bagno? for *where is the bathroom?*

Potrei avere un fazzoletto? for *may I have a tissue?*

Potrei avere un analgesico? for *may I have a painkiller?*

Ho bisogno di sgranchirmi le gambe for *I need to stretch my legs*

Non mi sento bene for *I don't feel well*

Ho freddo, ha una coperta per favore? for *I am cold, may I have a blanket please?*

Siete pregati di allacciare le cinture di sicurezza for *please, fasten your seatbelts*

La mia cuffia non funziona for *my headset does not work*

Sono previste turbolenze for *we are expecting turbulence*

Landing in Italy

Atterraggio for *landing*

Quanto manca all'atterraggio? for *how long before the landing?*

Quando atterreremo? for *when will we land?*

A che ora atterreremo? for *what time will we be landing?*

Saremo in ritardo/in anticipo for *ee will be late/early*

Saremo in ritardo/in anticipo? for *will we be late/early?*

Atterrare for *to land*

Siamo in fase di atterraggio for *we started landing*

L'aereo atterrerà tra mezz'ora for *the plane will land in half an hour*

Quando attereremo? For *when will we be landing?*

Dov'è il ritiro bagagli? for *where is the baggage claim?*

Controllo passaporti for *passport control*

The good news about landing in Italy is that you do not need to fill in any form on the plane before landing. They will still check your *passport/passports* (*passaporto/passaporti*) and you will still have to go through custom, where they will ask you if there is *anything* you need *to declare* (*qualcosa da dichiarare?*).

Il mio bagaglio è stato danneggiato for *my luggage has been damaged*

Il mio bagaglio è andato perso for *my luggage has been lost*

Ho perso il volo di coincidenza for *I missed my connection*

Ho perso il mio passaporto for *I lost my passport*

Ho perso il mio biglietto aereo for *I lost my ticket*

Ho perso la mia carta d'imbarco for *I lost my boarding card*

Mi sono perso for *I am lost*

How to leave the airport:

You can leave an airport in many different ways: taxi (*taxi*), shuttle (*shuttle*), busses (*bus*), train (*treno*), rental car (*macchina a noleggio*), steamboat (*vaporetto*).

You can find a taxi at the *taxi rank* (*parcheggio dei taxi*) right outside the airport, where you will probably also find all the shuttles and local busses. Local buses are very *inexpensive* (*economici*) and connect the airports with major cities, also with small towns, and may be the right choice for many locals. They are usually divided into *urban* (*urbano*) and *suburban* (*interurbano* or *extraurbano*) lines, and you might need to buy tickets in advance at the *newstand* (*il giornalaio*). Shuttles are usually quite efficient and drivers usually sell *tickets* (*biglietti*) themselves. Airport shuttles are highly developed and convenient for rail travelers and few airports (Roma Fiumicino, Milano Malpensa and Torino Caselle) are directly connected to the *railway network* (*rete ferroviaria*).

Taking off from Italy

When you are taking off from Italy, instead of landing, the main task is to wander the airport (*muoversi nell'aeroporto*), check in, go through security (*la sicurezza*), and board at the right gate. After some shopping (and alast Italian espresso!), you will probably be ready *to leave* (*partire*).

GRAMMAR TIP: the conjugation of *partire* (*to leave*) and *arrivare* (*to arrive*), present, past and future

The two most important verbs when traveling are *partire* (*to leave*) and *arrivare* (*to arrive*).

As a reminder, verbs end differently for different persons. In Italian, there are three possible infinitive endings or conjugations: -are, -ere, and -ire. The infinitive form of a verb (i.e. *partire* -*to leave*) loses its ending, which coincides with the last three letters (i.e., *-ire* for *partire*). You will always have the first part of the verb, like part- or arriv-, and then add the person. Persons are the same for verbs of the same conjugations, but may differ for persons of verbs belonging to different conjugations:

Voi arriv-ate for *you* (many) *arrive* is different from *voi corr-ete* for *you* (many) *run* and *voi part-ite* for *you* (many) *leave*.

Simple present of *partire* (*to leave*):

Io parto for *I leave*

Tu parti for you *leave*

Lei/lui parte for *she/he leaves*

Noi partiamo for *we leave*

Voi partite for *you leave*

Essi/loro partono for *they leave*

Present perfect* of ***partire*** (*to leave*):

Io sono partito for *I have left*

Tu sei partito for *you have left*

Lei è partita / lui è partito for *she/he has left*

Noi siamo partiti for *we have left*

Voi siete partiti for *you* (many) *have left*

Essi/loro sono partiti for *they have left*

The future of ***partire*** (*to leave*):

Io partirò for *I will leave*

Tu partirai for *you will leave*

Lei/lui partirà for *she/he will leave*

Noi partiremo for *we will leave*

Voi partirete for *you* (many) *will leave*

Essi/loro partiranno for *they will leave*

Simple present of ***arrivare*** (*to arrive*):

Io arrivo for *I arrive*

Tu arrivi for *you arrive*

Lei/lui arriva for *she/he arrive*

Noi arriviamo for *we arrive*

Voi arrivate for *you arrive*

Essi/loro arrivano for *they arrive*

Present perfect* of ***arrivare*** (*to arrive*):

Io sono arrivato for *I have arrived* (*I arrived*)

Tu sei arrivato for *you have arrived* (*you arrived*)

Lei è arrivata/lui è arrivato for *she/he has arrived* (*she/he arrived*)

Noi siamo arrivati for *we have arrived* (*we arrived*)

Voi siete arrivati for *you* (many) *have arrived* (*we arrived*)

Loro/essi sono arrivati for *they have arrived* (*they arrived*)

The future of *arrivare* (*to arrive*):

Io arriverò for *I will arrive*

Tu arriverai for *you will arrive*

Lei/lui arriverà for *she/he will arrive*

Noi arriveremo for *we will arrive*

Voi arriverete for *you* (many) *will arrive*

Loro/essi arriveranno for *they will arrive*

*In Italian, the present perfect is used more frequently (sometimes erroneously) as a past rather than a present perfect. And it happens that Italians would say *ho fatto* when you say *I did*, and *sono andato* when you say *I went*.

Trains

The majority of Italian trains and railway are owned and managed by a state company, *Le Ferrovie dello Stato* Italiane, and there are other (also public) regional agencies that operate on the Italian network. For both, it is possible to book trips and purchase tickets and passes online at trenitalia.com, which has a very functional English version.

High speed trains (*treni ad alta velocità*, AV -formerly Eurostar Italia) connect major cities, such as Roma, Firenze, Bologna, Milano, Torino, Venezia, Napoli, Salerno, within a few hours and are quite comfortable. A *reservation* (*prenotazione*) for an *assigned seat* (***posto assegnato***) is required for these trains at a small commission. There are three kinds of high speed trains, from the fastest: *il **Frecciarossa*** (*Red arrow*), *il **Frecciargento*** (*Silver arrow*), and *il **Frecciabianca*** (*White arrow*).

Intercity trains (***Intercity IC***) are the next fastest trains and connect cities and towns off the main network during the day. The *night trains* (***Intercity Notte ICN***) have sleeper compartments (***vagoni letto***) and washrooms (***bagni***), but no showers on board.

Regional services both fast (***regionale veloce RGV***) and slow (***regionale REG***) connect the smaller stations between cities. Trains of regional agencies are connected and shown on Trenitalia; their tickets can also be purchased at the local newsstand or tobacco store.

At the station

In almost every train station (***stazione dei treni***), no matter how big or small, there will be a *ticket booth* (***una biglietteria automatica***) where you can plan your trip, reserve a seat, buy your ticket or print a ticket you bought online. You are required *to stamp/validate* (***obliterare***) your ticket before getting on the train; otherwise, there is always the ticket inspector (***il controllore***) who will issue you a fine (***una multa***). The reason is that for regional services there is no date or time on the ticket and the same ticket could be used multiple times if not stamped. The only exception are the tickets with a seat reservation because they have a precise date for a determined train.

The *validating machines* (***le obliteratrici***) are usually located close by the ticket booth, before the *tracks* (***binari***) and on the *platform* (***la pensilina***).

Different panels by the tracks will show the *schedules* (***gli orari***) of the closest departures (***partenze***) and arrivals (***arrivi***). For every train, you will see the time and *platform* (***binario***).

You can always go to the *ticket office* (***biglietteria***) and speak with the *clerk* (***addetto***) if you want to make sure to have the right tickets for your destination.

Buongiorno, vorrei un biglietto di sola andata per Venezia Centrale

Good morning, I would like a one-way ticket for Venezia Centrale

Buongiorno vorremmo due biglietti di andata e ritorno per Roma Termini

Good morning, we would like two round trip tickets for Roma Termini

Local busses

Travel by bus in Italy lets you reach destinations which, due to Italy's geography, are not connected to the rail network. There are always regional public busses (*autobus interurbani*) which connect train stations, airports to cities (*città*), and small villages (*paesi*). You can buy the tickets for these busses either at the bus station (*stazione degli autobus*) or at a newsstand (*giornalaio*) of ticket booths (*biglietterie automatiche*) at the train station or at the airport. Often, not always, you can also buy the ticket on the bus. Other private bus providers offer low cost bus tickets, offering convenient connections with Italy and connecting Italy to many European destinations.

Car rentals

Public transportation in Italy is quite efficient, and while it is great, you still must stick to a schedule, and the busses and trains only take you so far. Renting a car (*noleggiare una macchina*) in Italy will provide you with the freedom of moving at your pleasure and is a wonderful way to see the country. You can drive up to the mountains (*montagne*), see quaint villages (*paesi pittoreschi*), drive past cliffside vineyards (*vigne*), find a random castle (*castello*), stop by the hidden beach (*spiaggia*) you would have otherwise never spotted, and more.

There are few things to remember when renting a car in Italy. You can book your car online, in English, and it will probably be cheaper.

Second, the majority of the rental cars have a standard shift with *manual transmission* (***cambio manuale***). If you need or want an *automatic* (***cambio automatico***), you need to specify and probably reserve it quite far in advance. As anywhere, you can find the major *rental companies* (***compagnie/agenzie di autonoleggio***), some European, and some Italian ones.

As anywhere else, you will have to choose which *kind of car* (***tipo di macchina***) you want, which may depend on where you are going, how *many suitcases* (***quante valigie***) you have, and how many *passengers* (***passeggeri***) there will be.

As far as the *insurance* (***assicurazione***) is concerned, you need to remember that the *deductible* (***franchigia***) is the limit or the most that the *insurance company* (***compagnia assicurativa***) will reimburse you in case of *damage* (***danno***). The rest of the amount will be on you. A more expensive option will cover the damage completely. This option is often referred to as ***kasko*** in Italy, even when provided by a different company.

Companies offer many different kinds of rentals: by *hour* (***orario***), by *day* (***giornaliero***), by *week* (***settimanale***), by month (***mensile***). You can even still choose between limited and unlimited miles (***chilometraggio limitato*** o ***illimitato***). Then you can choose to add some optional features to your rental: a *navigation system* (***sistema di navigazione***), the *prepay fuel* (***pieno prepagato***), a *car seat* (***seggiolino***) or a *booster* (***adattatore***).

Distances in Italy are measured in *meters* (***metri***) and *kilometers* (***chilometri***) rather than *feet* (***piedi***) and *miles* (***miglia***). Approximately, a *meter* (***un metro***) corresponds to *three feet* (***tre piedi***) and *one mile* (***un miglio***) corresponds to *one kilometer and a half* (***un chilometro e mezzo***). Exactly, *one foot* (***un piede***) is 0.3 meters (***metri***) and one mile equals 1.6 kilometers, so you will probably think places are further away than they really are if you are looking at their distance in kilometers.

If you do not choose prepaid fuel, you need to remember to *fill the tank* (*fare il pieno*) before returning your *rental car* (*macchina a noleggio*). The petrol/gas prices might look quite low, but keep in mind that in Italy—and pretty much the entire world—*gasoline* (*benzina*) is sold by the *liter* (*litro*) rather than the *gallon* (*gallone*). You need *four and a half liters* (*quattro litri e mezzo*) for one gallon. The price is quite variable in Italy as well—just remember that you might need four times more then what you expect to fill the tank! Also, there might be a pay station shared by a couple of numbered *pumps* (*pompe*), but it may only take debit cards (*bancomat*) and no credit cards (*carte di credito*). Usually, these machines take *cash* (*contanti*), though, in *bills* (*banconote*).

The usual speed limit in a *town* (*paese*) or *city* (*città*) or any populated area (*centro urbano*) is 50km/h, (i.e., *50 kilometers per hour – cinquanta chilometri all'ora*), which is 31 miles per hour. The *strade extraurbane secondarie* (*secondary state roads*) are main roads that connect cities, towns, and airports, and the usual speed limit is 90 km/h. These roads used to be called *strade statali* (*SS*), *strade regionali* (*SR*) or *strade provinciali* (*SP*), and they are all marked by one of those initials and a number. There are also *strada extraurbana principale* or *superstrade* (*principal state road* and Italian equivalent for expressway). These roads are directly controlled by the Italian government or by the regions—there is no toll and the general speed limit is 110 km/h. Access restrictions on these expressways are the same as those for *highways* (*autostrade*). Italian Highways (*autostrade italiane*) are marked with the letter A and a number, and are managed by the government (Ministero delle Infrastrutture e dei Trasporti) who impose a *toll* (*pedaggio*). There are two kinds of toll. The *closed toll system* (*a sistema chiuso*) is more common and requires one to take a ticket when entering the highway and to pay at the exit. The amount you will be charged is proportional to the distance you traveled, the vehicle you drove, and the highway you drove on. You can also purchase the automatic system (Telepass) that will detect your entrance and exit and automatically charge you and skip the lines. There is also an *open system* (*sistema aperto*) on few minor portions, by which everybody pays a fixed amount regardless of distance and vehicle. The speed limit on highways is normally 130 km/h (81 miles per hour), but varies with the weather and experience: with rain and snow it can reduce to 110 km/h, with fog to 50 km/h and new drivers need to drive with a 110km/h limit for three years.

Buongiorno vorrei noleggiare una macchina

Good morning I would like to rent a car

Buongiorno ho prenotato una macchina a noleggio

Good morning I reserved a rental car

Che tipo di macchina vorreste?

What kind of car would you like?

Waterways

Italy is a *peninsula* (*penisola*) with many *islands* (*isole*), and most of its borders are in the sea. Many ferries (*traghetti*) connect Italy with other countries: Spagna, Francia, Croazia, Grecia, Tunisia, Marocco, and Algeria are some of them. Plus a network of ferries and hydrofoils connect the islands and the mainland to the islands, like la Sicilia, la Sardegna, le Isole Eolie, le Isole Tremiti, le Isole Pontine, Pantelleria, Capri, Ischia, and l'Isola d'Elba. Also, major Cities, like Venezia, Genova, Napoli, and Trieste, are destination points for *cruises* (*crociere*).

GRAMMAR TIP: the conjugation of *imbarcarsi, to board*

When you travel by boat, as on a plane, you *board* (*imbarcarsi*)

Simple Present:

Io mi imbarco for *I board*

Tu ti imbarchi for *you board*

Lei/lui si imbarca for *she/he boards*

Noi ci imbarchiamo for *we board*

Voi vi imbarcate for *you* (many) *board*

Loro/essi si imbarcano for *they board*

Present perfect:

Io mi sono imbarcato for *I boarded*

Tu ti sei imbarcato for *you boarded*

Lei/lui si è imbarcato for *she/he boarded*

Noi ci siamo imbarcati for *we boarded*

Voi vi siete imbarcati for *you* (many) *boarded*

Essi/loro si sono imbarcati for *they boarded*

Future:

Io mi imbarcherò for *I will board*

Tu ti imbarcherai for *you will board*

Lei/lui si imbarcherà for *she/he will board*

Noi ci imbarcheremo for *we will board*

Voi vi imbarcherete for *you* (many) *will board*

Essi/loro si imbarcheranno for *they will board*

Essential vocabulary:

Viaggiare in nave for *to travel by boat*

Avere mal di mare for *to be seasick*

Sbarcare for *to disembark*

Imbarcarsi for *to embark*

Salpare for *to sail*

Porto for *port*

Darsena for *harbor*

Terminal traghetti for ferry terminal

Crociera for cruise

Traversata for crossing

Passeggero a piedi for foot passenger

Mare calmo for calm sea

Mare agitato for rough sea

Capitano for captain

Membro dell'equipaggio for member of the crew

Cabina for cabin

Ponte for deck

Ponte per le auto for car deck

Passerella for gangway

Banco delle informazioni for information desk

Scialuppa di salvataggio for lifeboat

Giubbotto di salvataggio for life jacket

Salvagente for life belt

Types of vessel (*tipi di imbarcazione*):

Traghetto (adibito a trasporto auto) for car ferry

Nave da crociera for cruise ship

Traghetto for ferry

Hovercraft for hovercraft

Barca a remi for rowboat

Barca a vela for sailboat

Veliero for sailing ship

Motoscafo for motorboat

Aliscafo for hydrofoil

Vaporetto *for steamboat or waterbus (in Venice)*

Zattera *for raft*

Sailing

If you decide *to go sailing* (**andare in barca a vela**), you may like to know a few essential words before *boarding* (**imbarcarsi**). The *starboard* is to the right (**tribordo**), and *port* to the left (**babordo**). The *bow* or front of a *boat* (**barca**) is called **prua**; the *stern*, **poppa**, and the *helm*, **timone**. When you take the helm (**stare al timone** or, figuratively, **prendere il comando**, *to take command*) as **capitano** and **navigatore**. The *crew* (**l'equipaggio**) may consist of one *sailor* (**marinaio**) or more (**marinai**), and they *hoist* (**issare**) and *lower* (**calare**) the *sails* (**le vele**) in *calm* (**mare calmo**) and *rough seas* (**mare mosso**). There may be a **mozzo** (*ship's boy*) or a **cambusa**, which could be either a *boat's galley* or the *on-board cook*.

On foot

In Italy, you will often find yourself walking around and looking for the next *museum* (**museo**), *café* (**caffè** or **bar**), *restaurant* (**ristorante**), *ice cream store* (**gelateria**), a particular *store* (**negozio**) and probably your *hotel* (**albergo**). You may also need to find your way within a building: a *shopping mall* (**centro commerciale**), a big museum, an *aquarium* (**acquario**) or an *airport* (**aeroporto**)!

You may ask where to find what you are looking for:

Mi scusi sa dov'è la stazione? for *excuse me, do you* (formal) *know where the station is?*

Scusa, sai dov'è la stazione? for *excuse me, do you* (informal) *know where the station is?*

Certo, la stazione è di fronte all'albergo for *of course, the station is in front of the hotel*

Your destination may be *far* (**lontano**) or *close by* (**vicino**) or simply *over there* (**laggiù**) as different adverbs of place indicate.

Location adverbs

Qui, **qua** for *here*

Lì, **là** for *there*

Vicino for near, close

Lontano for far

Di fronte for in front of

Davanti for facing, in front of

Dietro for behind

Accanto for next to

A destra for on the right

A sinistra for on the left

Dentro for inside

Fuori for outside

Sopra for on, above

Su for up, on

Sotto for under, below

Giù for down, under

Intorno for around

Via for away

Quassù for up here

Quaggiù for down here

Lassù for up there

Laggiù for down there

Qui vicino for close by

Lì vicino for over there

Qui sopra for up here

Qui sotto for down here

Lì sopra for up there

Lì sotto for down there

Lì in cima for on top over there

Lì in fondo for down there

Possible destinations that you might need to reach are:

Il museo for *the museum*

Il teatro for *the theater*

Il ristorante for *the restaurant*

Il bar for *the coffee shop*

La fermata dell'autobus for *the bus stop*

Il parcheggio dei taxi for *the taxis*

L'ospedale for *the hospital*

La farmacia for *the pharmacy*

La stazione della polizia for *the police station*

Il pronto soccorso for *the emergency room*

Asking for directions on the street

You might need to know how to ask for directions, to understand the directions and find your way. To do that you need a few words that point (**indicare**) to where things are (adverbs of place) and a few verbs that help you navigate (**andare**/*to go*, **proseguire**/*to continue*, **girare**/*to turn*, s**voltare**/*to turn*, **salire**/*to go up*, **scendere**/*to go down*, **tornare**/*to return*).

Mi scusi sa indicarmi...? for *excuse me, do you know how to point me to...?*

Mi scusi mi potrebbe indicare...? for *excuse me, could you* (formal) *point me to...?*

As you saw in Chapter 5, a polite way to ask a question is by using the conditional of *volere* (*to want*):

Mi scusi, vorrei andare... for *excuse me, I would like to go....*

Another possibility is to use *dovere* (*to have to*) to indicate that you need to go somewhere and you can either use it in the present simple, since you must go in that particular place, or you can use the conditional, if it is not absolutely necessary or if you need to go there but you still want to be polite:

Mi scusi, devo andare alla stazione... for *excuse me, I have to go to the station*

Mi scusi dovrei andare alla stazione.... for *excuse me, I should go to the station*

Deve andare prima a destra al primo semaforo e poi a sinistra alla farmacia

You have to turn right at the traffic light and then left at the pharmacy

GRAMMAR TIP: the conjugation of *dovere* (*to have*)

Dovere (*to have to*) is also very commonly use in giving directions: *deve girare prima a sinistra e poi a destra* (*you have to turn first left and then right*). So you may like to have its conjugation for the Simple Present and the Simple Present Conditional for every person (you may find the imperfect, the present perfect and the future in Chapter 14).

Simple Present

Io devo for *I have to*

Tu devi for *you have to*

Lei/lui deve for *she/he has to*

Noi dobbiamo for *we have to*

Voi dovete for *you* (many) *have to*

Essi/loro devono for *they have to*

Simple Present Conditional

Io dovrei for *I should*

Tu dovresti for *you should*

Lei/lui dovrebbe for *she/he should*

Noi dovremmo for *we should*

Voi dovreste for *you* (many) *should*

Essi/loro dovrebbero for *they should*

Mi scusi dovrei andare al museo d'arte moderna

Excuse me, I should go to the modern art museum

Deve andare sempre dritto fino alla stazione, poi deve girare a sinistra e proseguire per due isolati

You have to go straight until the station, then you have to turn left and keep going for two blocks

There might be more things that *you have to* (***tu devi***) to do in order to reach your destination:

Attraversare la strada for *to cross the street*

Prendere il sottopassaggio for *to take the underpassage*

Attraversare il ponte for *to cross the bridge*

In the unfortunate event that who is giving you directions will not use ***dovere*** followed by the infinite of one of the movement verbs, or that you want to repeat the directions to double-check whether you understood, you might need to know the Simple Present of the most common ones:

Simple present of ***andare*** (*to go*):

Io vado for *I go*

Tu vai for *you go*

Lei/lui va for *she/he goes*

Noi andiamo for *we go*

Voi andate for *you* (many) *go*

Essi/loro vanno for *they go*

Simple present of ***proseguire*** (*to continue*):

Io proseguo for *I continue*

Tu prosegui for *you continue*

Lei/lui prosegue for *she/he continue*

Noi proseguiamo for *we continue*

Voi proseguite for *you* (many) *continue*

Essi/loro proseguono for *they continue*

Simple Present of ***girare*** (*to turn*)

Io giro for *I turn*

Tu giri for *you turn*

Lei/lui gira for *she/he turns*

Noi giriamo for *we turn*

Voi girate for *you* (many) *turn*

Essi/loro girano for *they turn*

Asking for directions in a building

When inside a building, you might need a few more words to wander about on different floors and specific destinations:

Prendere l'ascensore for *to take the elevator*

Prendere le scale mobili for *to take the escalator*

Salire le scale for *to go up the stairwell*

Scendere le scale for *to go down the stairs*

Bus & Metro

Extensive metros (*metropolitane*) exist in Rome, Milan, Naples, and Turin, with smaller metros in Genoa and Catania. The *Minimetrò* in Perugia connects the train station with the city center.

Cities and towns of any size have an efficient **urbano** (*urban*) and **extraurbano** (*suburban*) bus system. Services are generally limited on Sundays and holidays.

Purchase bus and metro tickets before boarding and validate them once on board. Passengers with unvalidated tickets are subject to a fine (between €50 and €110). Buy tickets from a *tabaccaio* (tobacconist's shop), newsstands, ticket booths, or dispensing machines at bus and metro stations. Tickets usually cost around €1 to €2. Many cities offer good-value 24-hour or daily tourist tickets.

Taxi

You can catch a taxi at the official ranks outside most train and bus stations, or simply call for a radio taxi. Every city has its own company and different phone number. Radio taxi meters start running from when you have called rather than when you are picked up. Usually, taxi drivers accept *cash* (**contanti**) and do not have much *change* (**resto**). The best way to handle the destination is to have the precise address in Italian (possibly written). Extra charges are common for suitcases and trips outside the city border during the night. *A tip* (**una mancia**) may be nice, but not necessary; usually, it consists of a few euros or the change (*il resto*) if it is in that range.

Buongiorno vorrei andare in Via Roma 15

Good morning, I would like to go to Via Roma 15

Grazie, tenga il resto

I vaporetti di Venezia

A special case – Venice

Venezia (*Venice*) is built on an *archipelago* (*arcipelago*) of 118 islands (*isole*) connected by 400 bridges (*ponti*) over 177 canals (*canali*). The adjoining Ponte della Libertà and a railroad connect Venezia with the mainland. Beyond a parking facility (Piazzale Roma) and the train station (Venezia Santa Lucia), transportation is entirely on water or foot. This is the largest urban car-free area in Europe.

The classic Venetian boat is the *gondola* (plural: *gondole*), although it is now mostly used for tourists, or weddings, funerals, or other ceremonies, or as *traghetto/i* (*ferry/ferries*) to cross the Grand Canal instead of a nearby bridge.

The main public transportation means are motorized *waterbuses* (*vaporetti*), which use regular routes along the Grand Canal and between the city's islands. There are many authorized vendors in the historical centre of Venezia, where you can buy the tickets and learn about the routes.

Dove posso comprare i biglietti per il vaporetto? for *where can I buy the tickets for the waterbus?*

Quale vaporetto mi porta in Piazza San Marco? for *which waterbus takes me to Piazza San Marco?*

Quale vaporetto mi porta a Murano, Burano, e Torcello...? for *which waterbus takes me to Murano, Burano, and Torcello?*

Quale vaporetto va alla Biennale/ai Giardini? for *which waterbus goes to the Biennale/to I Giardini?*

Quando arriva il prossimo vaporetto? for *when does this waterbus arrive?*

Quanto tempo ci mette il vaporetto per andare all'aeroporto? for *how long does the waterbus take to get to the airport?*

Quanto spesso passa questo vaporetto per l'aeroporto? for *how often does the waterbus to airport come?*

Car

Driving around can be marvelous, whether you own or rent a car. You need to find parking and fill the tank at the gas station for *gas* (***benzina***). You might also have to go to the car wash. If something happens to the car, you might have to call a *tow truck* (***carro attrezzi***).

La strada for *the road*

La via for *the street*

La piazza for *the square*

Il semaforo for *traffic light*

La rotatoria for *rotary*

L'incrocio for *intersection*

Il vigile urbano for *traffic policeman*

L'isolato for *block*

La stazione di servizio for *service station*

L'autolavaggio for *car wash*

Vai dritto for *go straight*

Gira/svolta a destra for *turn right*

Gira/svolta a sinistra for *turn left*

Inverti la marcia for *reverse*

Fai retromarcia/fai marcia indietro for *reverse*

Fai un'inversione ad U for *take a U-turn*

Torna indietro for *go back*

Alla rotatoria prendi la prima, seconda, terza, quarta... uscita for *at the rotary, take the first, second, third, fourth... exit*

Prendi la prima strada a destra for *take the first street on the right*

Al semaforo gira a sinistra for *at the traffic light turn left*

Chapter 7 - Visiting

*Hotels (**albergo, alberghi**)*

When you arrive in Italy, you might just want to get to *your hotel room* (*la tua stanza d'albergo*) to take a shower (*doccia*) and a nap (*pisolino*). Hotels in Italy work as in the rest of the world. There are different kinds of hotels marked with more or less stars (*stelle*), and different kinds of *rooms* (*stanze*) for different budgets. Some may have *swimming pools* (*piscina, piscine*), *gyms* (*palestra, palestre*), *free breakfast* (*colazione inclusa*), a *restaurant* (*ristorante*) and an *in-house bar* (*bar*). Others may not even have an *elevator* (*ascensore*).

Usually, though, a *single room* (*stanza singola*) is for one person only, *a double room for single use* (*stanza doppia a uso singolo*) is a room that is big enough for two people, but since only one person is using it, there is a lower price. A double room of any kind is for two people, but double bedrooms often have two *twin beds* (*letti singoli*), which can be made up as two beds or put together to make a king-size bed. If a room has one *double bed* (*letto doppio*), it is usually queen-size. Rooms never have two double beds as is common in the USA.

*Small hotel (**pensione**)*

A smaller, family owned and managed hotel is traditionally called *pensione*. They usually have a cozy warm atmosphere, and there is a less formal relationship between hosts (*albergatore*) and guests (*ospite, ospiti*). Traditionally, the only option would have been to have one meal per day (*mezza pensione*), but even these kinds of accommodations have evolved and offer, nowadays, more comforts, like a spa or gym, etc.

*Hostels (**ostello, ostelli**)*

Hostels are a good option if you do not mind *sharing (**condividere**)*. Though, these facilities (both around the world and in Italy) have moved from strictly *dorm-style (**stile dormitorio**) bunks (**letti a castello**)* only for young people to historical buildings with smaller or private rooms with separate bathrooms and no age restrictions. If so, you still have the opportunity to use a shared kitchen (***cucina***) and living space (***salotto***). A hostel should offer accommodation on a budget, with the possibility of creating a familiar atmosphere among the guests.

Bed and Breakfasts

Bed and Breakfasts in Italy do not traditionally have a great reputation: many cheap hotels call themselves B&Bs if they include some kind of breakfast (***colazione***) in the price of the room. If you are really looking for the more traditional version of a B&B, you will want to find out exactly what breakfast consists of. Some Italian B&Bs serve nothing more than a typical Italian breakfast: *caffè e pasticcini* or *pane e marmellata* (coffee and pastry or bread and jam). Since Italians are not generally a breakfast culture, they are not exactly splashing out a big breakfast spread. You might find a fridge in your room stocked with *fruit (**frutta**), yogurt (**yogurt**)*, and the makings for coffee, or you may find some pastry and bread and jam in a common area and that will be the *breakfast* portion. You may book a B&B and then find it is really just a budget hotel that provides a simple buffet breakfast.

Agriturismo (farm holiday)

The usual translation for **agriturismo** (*farm holiday*) may be misleading. *Agriturismo* is a special kind of accommodation offered in a family-owned farm, where you can enjoy the food produced by the farm and activities especially organized for the guests. You might be able to go camping, enjoy locally produced food, oil or wine tasting (**degustazioni**), go trekking, horseback riding, kayaking, canoeing, etc. Often the accommodation is quite similar to a bed and breakfast, with a private room (**stanza singola** or **doppia** *–single* or *double room*) and a *shared bathroom* (**bagno condiviso**), usually with at least one *meal* (**pasto incluso**) per day.

*Convents and Monasteries (**conventi** e **monasteri**)*

Historically, Italy has been largely a Catholic country and unsurprisingly is full of convents and monasteries, some of which have a long history of opening their doors to *pilgrims* (**pellegrini**)— and for some, that has a modern twist. Some convents and monasteries now play host to not only pilgrims but *travelers* (**viaggiatori**) of any sort. You can find these kinds of accommodations both in cities and in the countryside, and they are often incredibly *cheap* (**economici**). They are also notoriously safe places to stay, which used to be very appealing to female travelers (either **pellegrine** or **viaggiatrici**). There might be few catches— staying in a convent can include having a *curfew* (**coprifuoco**), participating in *prayer times* (**preghiere**), or separate sleeping quarters for men and women.

*Villas and Other Vacation Rentals (**Ville** e **altri affitti per le vacanze**)*

If you decide on a longer stay or are part of a larger group (especially with young kids), you might like to rent a *house* (**casa**), an *apartment* (**appartamento**) or a *villa* (**villa**).

Camping (***campeggio***)

Camping is very popular in Italy with a very large number of official sites (*campeggio*) in operation, where you can stay for a nominal fee (***tassa giornaliera***), usually charged per person daily. A complete list of camping sites with a location map is issued free by the Federazione Italiana del Campeggio e del Caravanning (Federcampeggio).

Dining and drinking

In Italy, there are three main meals: *la prima colazione* (*breakfast*), *il pranzo* (*lunch*), and *la cena* (*dinner*). After these, children usually have a *snack* (***una merenda***) in the *morning* (***al mattino***) and or in the *afternoon* (***pomeriggio***). As an adult, you may need a *break* (***una pausa***) for a *coffee* (***caffè***) or *tea* (***tè*** or ***the***) in the morning and/or in the afternoon, or you might like to have an *aperitif* (***aperitivo***) before dinner.

Usually, breakfast is served from 7 a.m. till 9 a.m., lunch from 12 p.m. to 2 p.m. (or 14:00) and dinner from 7 till 11 p.m. (23:00) at least. In between, you may have a snack in pastry shops or a cafè.

The traditional Italian breakfast at home is *bread and jam* (***pane e marmellata***) with *coffee* (***caffè***)—often it is *bread* (***pane***), *butter* (***burro***), and *jam* (***marmellata***), and there is *milk* (***latte***) in the coffee, so to have a ***caffellatte***. It is possible to have breakfast at a bar. An Italian bar is not a pub or bar in the American sense; it is more like a small coffee shop, where you can have an espresso (and every possible variation), tea, sodas, and pastries. Many like to have their breakfast at the bar, and the standard is an *espresso* (***un caffè***) with a *croissant* (***cornetto***).

You can find a *continental breakfast* (***colazione continentale*** or ***colazione all'americana***) almost anywhere and you can order *eggs* (***uova***) *scrambled* (***strapazzate***), *fried* (***fritte***), or *hard-boiled* (***sode***) with or without *a piece of toasted bread* (***una fetta di pane tostato***).

You might also find *pancakes* (***frittelle***), *cereals* (***i cereali***), *yogurt,* and *seasonal fruit* (***frutta di stagione***).

Colazione *(la colazione, le colazioni)* for *breakfast*

Caffè *(il caffè, i caffè)* for *coffee*

Zucchero *(lo zucchero)* for *sugar*

Latte *(il latte)* for *milk*

Panna *(la panna)* for *cream*

Tè *(il tè)* for *tea*

Tazzina *(la tazzina, le tazzine)* for *small cup*

Tazza *(la tazza, le tazze)* for *cup*

Miele *(il miele)* for *honey*

Cornetto *(il cornetto, i cornetti)* for *croissant*

Cereali *(i cereali)* for *cereals*

Biscotti *(il biscotto, i biscotti)* for *cookies*

There are many different places where you can have lunch and dinner. The *restaurant* (***ristorante***) is a formal place that may or may not specialize in a particular kind of food, like those that mainly serve *fish* (***ristorante di pesce***) or *meat* (***ristorante di carne***) or *vegetarian food* (***ristorante vegetariano***). ***Trattorie*** are less formal venues with authentic regional food, which used to be a family-owned version of a diner. A ***pizzeria*** usually has a *brick oven* (***forno a legna***) and serves mainly pizza, but you can also find the main traditional Italian dishes. Sometimes, on the road, there are small shops where you can find ***pizza al taglio*** (*pizza by the slice*). In those places, you can either eat it quickly there standing or take it to go. ***Osteria*** is the closest to a tavern or corner pub, serving snacks, appetizers, simple dishes, and wine in an unpretentious venue. Although, if you would like to have a good *glass of wine* (***bicchiere di vino***) and eat some delicatessen, you might have better luck in an ***Enoteca***. Enoteca literally means "collection of wine", and in these venues, you can buy bottles of wine or just enjoy a few glasses of your choice.

Instead, if you are out in the country, you may decide to stop by an *agriturismo*, a farm that the owners have decided to partially use for accommodation purposes. There you will only find food made from the produce, eggs, meat, and often wine and olive oil that is fresh off the farm.

A *paninoteca* is the Italian answer to American fast food. It literally means "collection of *sandwiches* (*panini*)" and this is the main theme, but you are not expected to eat fast and go, and everything will be cooked and made on the spot. A *Rosticceria* sells whole rotisserie chickens and a variety of ready-to-eat meals for takeout at a fair price. There are also establishments (*tavola calda*) where you can find pre-made dishes (often local specialties); these are usually self-serve, cafeteria-style venues.

Lastly, when looking for a snack or a dessert after dinner, you can always stop by a homemade *ice-cream parlor* (*Gelateria*).

Ordering food

Restaurants, osterie, pizzerie, and so on usually do not have different *menus* (*menù*) for lunch and dinner. Either way, menus are usually divided in sections that reflect the course of an Italian meal: *antipasto* (appetizer), *primi* (*first courses*), *secondi* (*second courses*), *contorni* (*side dishes*), *frutta* (*fruit*), *dolci* (*dessert*). Appetizers may be *warm* (*caldi*) or *cold* (*freddi*), usually the cold ones are not cooked. *The first course* (*il primo*) might be further divided into *soups* (*zuppe* or *minestre*), rice dishes (*risotti*), and *pasta dishes* (*pasta*). *The second course* (*il secondo*) may also have subsections for *meat* (*carne*) and *fish* (*pesce*).

In the unfortunate event that the English menu went missing or you would like to try ordering from the Italian menu, here is some essential "menu vocabulary":

Essential vocabulary

Menù for *menu*

Antipasto for *appetizer*

Primi piatti for *first course*

Zuppa for *soup*

Minestra for *soup*

Brodo for *broth*

Secondi piatti for *second course*

Contorni for *side dishes*

Insalata for *salad*

Verdure for *vegetables*

Verdure grigliate for *grilled vegetables*

Verdure al forno for *baked vegetables*

Patate (la patata, le patate) for *potatoes*

Pesce (il pesce, i pesci) for *fish*

Trota (la trota, le trote) for *trout*

Salmone (il salmone, i salmoni) for *salmon*

Aragosta (l'aragosta, le aragoste) for *lobster*

Branzino (il branzino, i branzini) for *European Seabass*

Gambero (il gambero, i gamberi) for prawn or shrimp

Polpo or *Polipo* for *octopus*

Spada (pesce spada) for *swordfish*

Tonno (il tonno, i tonni) for *tuna*

Carne (la carne, le carni) for *meat*

Manzo for *beef*

Cinghiale for *boar*

Pollo for *chicken*

Tacchino for *turkey*

Coniglio for *rabbit*

Selvaggina for *game*

Going shopping

Like in the rest of the world, you can buy almost everything everywhere and find clothes in supermarkets or food in bookstores. However, in Italy, you can still find many specialized stores that will sell only what they were traditionally meant to sell. There are stores dedicated to *general food* (*i negozi di generi alimentari*) or specialize in a particular kind of food:

Macelleria (la macelleria, le macellerie) for *the butcher*

Pescheria (la pescherie, le pescherie) for *the fish market*

Salumeria (la salumeria, le salumerie) for *cold cuts, cheese, olives*

Fruttivendolo (il fruttivendolo, i fruttivendoli) for *fruit and vegetables*

Pasticceria (la pasticceria, le pasticcerie) for *bakery* for pastry

Panetteria (la panetteria, le panetterie) for *bakery* for bread and cookies

Panificio (il panificio, i panifici) for *bakery* for bread and cookies

Fornaio (il fornaio, i fornai) for *bakery* for bread and cookies

Enoteca (l'enoteca, le enoteche) for *wine dealer*

And more stores:

Tabaccheria (la tabaccheria, le tabaccherie) for *tobacco shop*

Libreria (la libreria, le librerie) for *book store*

Cartoleria (la cartoleria, le cartolerie) for *stationary store*

82

Profumeria (la profumeria, le profumerie) for *perfume store*

Negozio di abbigliamento (il negozio, i negozi) for *store for clothing*

Farmacia (la farmacia, le farmacie) for *pharmacy*

Drogheria (la drogheria, le drogherie) for *drugstore*

Just remember—when leaving a store, as you would do in English—to say: **Grazie e arrivederci** (*thank you, see you soon*) or **Grazie e buona giornata** (*thank you and have a good day*).

Groceries

If you need to buy groceries (**fare la spesa**), you can choose to go to the *supermarket* (**il supermercato**) and fill your *basket* (**cestino**) or *cart* (**il carrello**) with all sorts of goods. Either way, when you buy by weight, you need to remember that Italy, like most of the world, uses the metric system. In the metric system, you have *grams* (**grammi**), *dekagrams* or ten grams (**decagrammo**), *hectograms* or 100 grams (**ettogrammo**), and *kilograms* or 1000 grams (**chilogrammo**). Usually, for groceries, grams and kilograms are used. One *pound* (*libbra*) is approximately 454 *grams* (**grammi**), so every time that you ask for a *kilo* (**un chilo**) you will receive two pounds; or if you really need just a pound, you can ask for *half a kilo* (**mezzo chilo**).

After you collect everything you need, you must pay at the *register* (*la cassa*). Nowadays, cash, debit, and credit cards are accepted; but there may be a *minimum amount* (**importo minimo**) required to use the credit card. You might be surprised by a few things in an Italian supermarket. You have to bag your groceries, and possibly quite quickly. As of a few years ago, you needed to bring your bags (**borse della spesa**). In case they still have plastic bags (**buste di plastica**), you must pay for each one and you might have to tell the cashier how many you need before they start scanning your groceries.

Mi scusi vorrei un chilo di... for *excuse me I would like a kilo of...*

Dal fruttivendolo (*fruit and vegetable store*):

Frutta *(la frutta)* for *fruit*

Verdura *(la verdura, le verdure)* for *vegetable*

Pompelmo *(il pompelmo, i pompelmi)* for *grapefruit*

Carota *(la carota, le carote)* for *carrot*

Cavolfiore *(il cavolfiore, i cavolfiori)* for *cauliflower*

Ciliegia *(la ciliegia, le ciliegie)* for *cherry*

Fungo *(il fungo, i funghi)* for *mushroom*

Cetriolo *(il cetriolo, i cetrioli)* for *cucumber*

Limone *(il limone, i limoni)* for *lemon*

Sedano *(il sedano)* for *celery*

Albicocca *(l'albicocca, le albicocche)* for *apricot*

Melone *(il melone, i meloni)* for *melon*

Anguria *(l'anguria, le angurie)* for *watermelon*

Cipolla *(la cipolla, le cipolle)* for *onion*

Cavolo *(il cavolo, i cavoli)* for *cabbage*

Pesca *(la pesca, le pesche)* for *peach*

Lattuga *(la lattuga)* for *lettuce*

Piselli *(il pisello, i piselli)* for *peas*

Pomodoro *(il pomodoro, i pomodori)* for *tomato*

Patata *(la patata, le patate)* for *potatoes*

Spinaci *(lo spinacio, gli spinaci)* for *spinach*

Fagiolini *(i fagiolini)* for *green beans*

Zucca *(la zucca, le zucche)* for *pumpkin*

Ananas *(l'ananas, gli ananas)* for *pineapple*

Susina *(la susina, le susine)* for *plum*

Fragola *(la fragola, le fragole)* for *strawberry*

Mirtillo *(il mirtillo, i mirtilli)* for *blueberry*

Uva *(l'uva)* for *grapes*

Arancia *(l'arancia, le arance)* for *orange*

Pera *(la pera, le pere)* for *pear*

Mela *(la mela, le mele)* for *apple*

In macelleria (*at the butcher*):

Carne *(la carne)* for *meat*

Pollo *(il pollo)* for *chicken*

Tacchino for *turkey*

Manzo for *beef*

Maiale for *pork*

Fettina *(la fettina, le fettine)* for *cutlet*

Petto *(il petto, i petti)* for *breast*

Coscia *(la coscia, le cosce)* for *thigh*

Bistecca *(la bistecca, le bistecche)* for *steak*

Macinata for *ground meat*

In salumeria (*delicatessen*):

Salame for *salami*

Prociutto cotto for *ham*

Prociutto crudo for *prosciutto*

Olive *(l'oliva, le olive)* for *olives*

Formaggio (il formaggio, i formaggi) for *cheese*

Negozio di alimentari (*in a grocery store*):

Olio for *oil*

Aceto for *vinegar*

Uova for *eggs*

Yogurt for *yogurt*

Scatoletta (la scatoletta, le scatolette) for *can*

Pharmacy and drugstore

Pharmacies and drugstores in Italy are separated, and whereas you can find a drugstore section in a supermarket, you cannot find a *pharmacy* (*farmacia*) in either a supermarket or drugstore. Italian pharmacies have their own standing in Italy. This is where you buy your medications, either with or without a prescription. Sometimes you can find high-end products (*prodotti*) for *personal hygiene* (*igiene personale*) or *beauty products* (*prodotti di bellezza*).

Buongiorno, ho mal di testa, ho bisogno di un analgesico

Good morning, I have a headache, I need some painkillers

Buongiorno, ho mal di denti, avete dei buoni antidolorifici?

Good morning, I have a toothache, do you have good painkillers?

Many translate drugstore with *drogheria*—it sounds like it, but these are two very different kinds of stores. *Una drogheria* used to be a store where you could find spices (*spezie*) by bulk, basic food, and other useful products for the house (like detergents, dish-soap, etc), but also for personal hygiene (like shampoo or a razor). When you need a special personal product, like makeup, perfume, or aftershave, you need to go to a *perfume shop* (*profumeria*). Nowadays you find these two kinds of stores merged in something very similar to an American drugstore and can be called either way (*drogheria* or *profumeria*), where you can find house and personal products.

Essential vocabulary:

Detersivo (il detersivo, i detersivi) for *detergents*

Detergenti (il detergente, i detergenti), for *cleanser*

Trucco *(il trucco, i trucchi)* for *makeup*

Rossetto *(il rossetto, i rossetti)* for *lipstick*

Mascara *(il mascara, i mascara)* for *mascara*

Cipria *(la cipria)* for *face powder*

Fondotinta *(il fondotinta, i fondotinta)* for *foundation*

Crema *(la crema, le creme)* for *lotion*

Crema solare for *sun lotion*

Pettine *(il pettine, i pettini)* for *comb*

Smalto *(lo smalto, gli smalti)* for *nail polish*

Dentifricio *(il dentifricio, i dentifrici)* for *toothpaste*

Spazzolino da denti *(lo spazzolino, gli spazzolini)* for *toothbrush*

Fazzoletti di carta for *tissue paper*

Spazzola *(la spazzola, le spazzole)* for *brush*

Cerotti *(il cerotto, i cerotti)* for *band-aid*

Disinfettante *(il disinfettante, i disinfettanti)* for *disinfectant*

Clothes

There are different kinds of stores you might want to visit for your shopping (*le spese*): you can go to a *mall* (*centro commerciale*) with many different *stores* (*negozi*), to a *department store* (*grandi magazzini*) or you can walk through the town or city center (*il centro*) and pick your little local store (*negozio*) or fancy boutique (*boutique*). You are looking for *something elegant* (*qualcosa di elegante*) and *formal* (*formale*) or *casual* (*casual* or *sportivo*) and *informal* (*informale*).

Depending on which kind of store you decide to visit, you may (or may not) find somebody willing to help, a *shop assistant* (*un commesso* or *una commessa*). You might want to try whether the clothes you like *fit* you (*andare bene**) and *suit* you (*stare bene**), and you need to look for the *dressing room* (**camerino di prova**) or *dressing rooms* (**camerini di prova**).

Before choosing what to try on, you might need to pause and realize that *Italian sizes* (**le taglie italiane**) maight be different from what you expect. For example, for a dress, a US *small* or 2-4 (**taglia piccola**) corresponds to an Italian 38-40, a US *medium* (**taglia media**) corresponds to a 42-44, a US *large* (**taglia grande**) corresponds to a 46-48, and so on. Although, nowadays, all this information might be found on the label. Either way, you may ask the *shop assistant* (**commesso**) to look for a *different size* (**un'altra taglia**) for you, either *smaller* (**più piccola**) or *bigger* (**più grande**).

Maybe you will just browse (**dare un'occhiata***) or *look for* (**cercare**) something in particular, or you might *need* to buy something (**aver bisogno***), or you might have seen something in the *window* (**la vetrina**).

Mi scusi, sto cercando un... for *excuse me, I am looking for...*

Mi scusi, avrei bisogno di... for *excuse me, I would need...*

Mi scusi, quanto costa quella camicia? for *excuse me, how much is that shirt?*

Mi scusi vorrei provare quella gonna for *excuse me, I would like to try on that skirt*

Vorrei provare questo vestito, ma ho bisogno di una taglia media for *I would like to try on this dress, but I need a medium size*

Mi scusi, potrebbe portarmi la taglia più piccola? for *excuse me could you bring me a smaller size?*

Some verbs that might help while looking for clothes:

Cercare for *to look for*

Mettersi for *to put on*

Togliersi for *to take off*

Provare for *to try on*

Vestirsi for *to get dressed*

Guardare le vetrine for *window shopping*

Costare for *to cost*

Pagare for *to pay*

Some essential words to go clothes shopping:

Calzini *(il calzino, i calzini)* for *socks*

Mutande *(la mutanda, le mutande)* for *underwear*

Canottiera *(la canottiera, le canottiere)* for *undershirt*

Pantaloni *(i pantaloni)* for *trousers*

Jeans *(i jeans)* for *jeans*

Maglietta *(la maglietta, le magliette)* for *T-shirt*

Gonna *(la gonna, le gonne)* for *skirt*

Camicia *(la camicia, le camicie)* for *button-down shirt*

Camicetta *(la camicetta, le camicette)* for *blouse*

Cravatta *(la cravatta le cravatte)* for *tie*

Pantaloncini *(i pantaloncini)* for *shorts*

Collant *(i collant)* for *tights, pantyhose*

Vestito *(il vestito, i vestiti)* for *dress*

Maglione *(il maglione, i maglioni)* for *sweater*

Felpa *(la felpa, le felpe)* for *sweatshirt*

Cardigan *(il cardigan, i cardigan)* for *cardigan*

Sciarpa *(la sciarpa, le sciarpe)* for *scarf*

Guanti *(il guanto, i guanti)* for *gloves*

Cintura *(la cintura, le cinture)* for *belt*

Cerniera lampo *(la cerniera, le cerniere)* for *zipper*

Bottoni *(il bottone, i bottoni)* for *button*

Tasca *(la tasca, le tasche)* for *pocket*

Cappotto *(il cappotto, i cappotti)* for *coat*

Giacca *(la giacca, le giacche)* for *jacket*

Ombrello *(l'ombrello, gli ombrelli)* for *umbrella*

Giubbotto *(il giubbotto, i giubbotti)* for *windbreaker*

Berretto *(il berretto, i berretti)* for *cap*

Cappello *(il cappello, i cappelli)* for *hat*

Sottoveste *(la sottoveste, le sottovesti)* for *slip*

Reggiseno *(il reggiseno, i reggiseno)* for *bra*

Borsa *(la borsa, le borse)* for *handbag*

Borsetta *(la borsetta, le borsette)* for *purse*

Mutandina *(la mutandina, le mutandine)* for *panties*

Impermeabile *(l'impermeabile, gli impermeabili)* for *raincoat*

*   **Andare bene** (*to fit*) and **stare bene** (*to suit*) are two verbal expressions made with **andare** (*to go*) or **stare** (*to stay*) followed by **bene** (*well*). In the same way, **avere bisogno** (*to need*) follows the normal conjugation of **avere,** followed by **bisogno** (*need*), and **dare un'occhiata** is formed by **dare** (*to give*) and **un'occhiata** (*a gaze*). You can find the conjugations of these verbs in Chapter 14 – Essential Grammar.

Shoes

You might need or want to buy a *pair of shoes* (**paio di scarpe**) and decide to go for either a big or small store. As for the clothes, Italy has its own system; but differently from clothes, the size of a shoe is a "measure": **misura**. *For men* (**da uomo**), *sizes* (**misure**) go from about 39 (US 7) to 45 (US11), and *for women* (**da donna**), sizes usually range from 35 (US 5) to 40 (US 9).

Scarpe da uomo for *men shoes*

Scarpe da donna for *women shoes*

Scarpe da bambino for *children shoes*

Scarpa destra for *right shoe*

Scarpa sinistra for *left shoe*

Dita del piede for *toes*

Tallone for *heel (of the foot)*

Arco del piede for *arch*

Tacco for *heel (of the shoe)*

Stivali *(lo stivale, gli stivali)* for *boots*

Sandali *(il sandalo, i sandali)* for *sandals*

Ballerine *(la ballerina, le ballerine)* for *ballet shoes*

Scarpe da ginnastica for *sneakers*

Mocassini for *loafers*

Infradito for *flip flops*

Pantofole for *slippers*

Books, gifts, and souvenirs

You may like to buy something for yourself or somebody else, and for this, you might need to go to different stores. You can buy *books* (***libri***) in a *bookstore* (***una libreria***), or a *pen* (***penna***), *pencil* (***matita***) or *stationery* (***carta da lettere***) in a *stationery store* (***cartoleria***).

If you need something more precious, you may go to a *jewelry store* (***una gioielleria***), where you can find a *silver bracelet* (***braccialetto d'argento***) or a *golden necklace* (***collana d'oro***), or a *platinum ring* (***anello di platino***) or a *brooch* (***spilla***), or a *pair of earrings* (***paio di orecchini***). You might also find a very nice *wrist watch* (***orologio da polso***), but you may have more options at a *watch seller* (*orologiaio*), where they can fix (*riparare*) yours in case something happened.

Dry cleaners

Traditionally, in Italy, you would find a *dry cleaner* (*lavanderia a secco*) rather than a *laundromat* (*lavanderia a gettoni* or *lavanderia automatica*). These, however, are becoming more and more popular. At the laundromat, you will find both a *washer* (*lavatrice*) and *dryer* (*asciugatrice*), which is quite uncommon to find in an average household. You will need to bring along a *detergent* (*detergente*) and *softener* (*ammorbidente*). Hopefully, your hotel will have a *laundry service* (*un servizio lavanderia*), and, hopefully, you will be satisfied, or you will have *to complain* (*lamentarsi*).

Hairdresser and the barber

It is not recommended that you go to a hairdresser with a language barrier, but you might want or need to be brave and try to have a haircut or treat yourself to a full service makeover while on vacation. The first odd thing you will notice is that *hair* is always plural in Italian: *capelli*. This is why, sometimes, Italians say that they brushed their *hairs* when they really brushed their *hair*.

Vorrei un taglio di capelli for *I would like to get a haircut*

Li vorrei corti for *I would like it short*

Li voglio tenere abbastanza lunghi for *I would like to keep it quite long*

Vorrei lisciarli for *I would like to make it straight*

Vorrei fare una permanente for *I would like a perm*

Li vorrei biondi for *I would like it blond*

Li vorrei scuri for *I would like it dark*

Li vorrei rossi, blu, verdi... for *I would like it red, blue, green...*

Post Office

More likely, you might need to find a post office to send a *letter* (***lettera***), *post card* (***cartolina***) or *package* (***pacco*** or ***pacchetto***). Although, you can buy stamps at the *tobacco store* (***tabaccaio***) and, usually, there are many *mailboxes* (***cassette delle lettere***) around cities and towns. Nevertheless, you may need to *stay in line* (***fare la fila***) and speak to a *clerk* (*impiegato postale*) to send a *package* (***pacco***) to yourself, your family, or a friend.

Optometrist

In case you wear glasses or contacts, you might need to go to a store to fix your glasses, buy new ones, or buy contacts. You might not be required to have a *test* (***esame della vista***) or *prescription* (***prescrizione***) to do so and the system is the same:

Buongiorno, mi si sono rotti gli occhiali for *good morning my glasses broke*

Buon giorno, vorrei comprare delle lenti a contatto for *good morning I would like to buy some contacts*

I suoi occhiali saranno pronti domani for *your glasses will be ready tomorrow*

Può ritirare i suoi occhiali nel pomeriggio for *you can pick up your glasses in the afternoon*

Montatura (la montatura, le montature) for *frame*

Lente (la lente, le lenti) for *lens*

Prezzo (il prezzo, i prezzi) for *price*

Riparazione (la riparazione, le riparazioni) for *repair*

Doctor and Dentist

Unfortunately, things happenm and you might need to *see a doctor* (***andare dal dottore***) or *dentist* (***andare dal dentista***):

Mi sento male for *I feel bad*

Mi gira la testa for *I feel dizzy*

Mi fa male lo stomaco for *I have a stomachache*

Ho la febbre for *I have a fever*

Ho un raffreddore for *I have a cold*

Mi viene da vomitare for *I feel like vomiting*

Piede (il piede, i piedi) for *foot*

Gamba (la gamba, le gambe) for *leg*

Dito (il dito, le dita) for *finger*

Mano (la mano, le mani) for *hand*

Braccio (il braccio, le braccia) for *arm*

Collo (il collo, i colli) for *neck*

Faccia (la faccia, le facce), for *face*

Bocca (la bocca, le bocche) for *mouth*

Occhio (l'occhio, gli occhi) for *eyes*

Orecchio (l'orecchio, gli orecchi) for *ear*

Mi fa male un dente for *my tooth hurts*

Apra la bocca for *open your mouth*

Risciaqui la bocca for *rinse your mouth*

Cavare un dente for *to extract a tooth*

Curare una carie for *to fix a cavity*

Sostituire una piombatura for *to change a filling*

Chapter 8 - Language and Culture

Much had been said about how much you can learn about a culture when you learn its language or languages: you learn about how they think while you learn how they speak. There are two kinds of expressions that deliver so much of a culture that they are sometimes, unfortunately, the last to be learned. These are proverbs, which are old familiar sayings supposedly carrying pearls of practical wisdom (*perle di saggezza*), and idiomatic expressions (*espressioni idiomatiche*), whose meanings do not match the literal meaning of the words they are made up with. Idioms especially are very frequent, and just knowing a few of them might help you navigate everyday life in Italy quite a lot:

Verbs – idiomatic expressions

Stare zitta for *to be quiet*

Stare attento for *to pay attention*

Stare con qualcuno for *to be in a relationship with*

Stare fermo for *to keep still*

Stare fuori for *to be outside*

Stare a pennello for *to fit like a glove*

Stare in guardia for *to be on one's guard*

Stare in piedi for *to be standing*

Fare apposta for *to do something on purpose*

Fa bel tempo for *it is good weather*

Fa cattivo tempo for *it is bad weather*

Fare il biglietto for *to buy a ticket*

Fare la colazione for *to have breakfast*

Fare i compiti for *to do homework*

Fare di tutto for *to do everything possible*

Fare una domanda for *to ask a question*

Fare la fila/la coda for *to stand in line*

Fare finta (di) for *to pretend*

Fare una fotografia for *to take a picture*

Fare ginnastica for *to exercise*

Fare una gita for *to go on an excursion*

Fare male for *to be painful, to ache*

Fare da mangiare for *to cook*

Fare passare for *to let through*

Fare una passeggiata for *to take a walk*

Fare il pieno (di benzina) for *to fill the gas tank*

Fare presto for *to hurry, to be quick*

Fare alla romana for *to split the check*

Fare la spesa for *to go grocery shopping*

Fare le spese for *to go shopping*

Fare tardi for *to be late*

Fare la valigia for *to pack the suitcase*

Far vedere for *to show something to somebody*

Fare un viaggio for *to take a trip*

Fare visita for *to visit*

Farsi il bagno for *to take a bath*

Farsi la doccia for *to take a shower*

Farsi la barba for *to shave*

Avere bisogno di for to need

Avere caldo for *to be warm*

Avere fame for *to be hungry*

Avere fortuna for *to be lucky*

Avere freddo for *to be cold*

Avere fretta for *to be in a hurry*

Avere paura for *to be afraid*

Avere ragione for *to be right*

Avere sete for *to be thirsty*

Avere sonno for *being sleepy*

Avere voglia di for *to want* or *to feel like*

Avere il mal di mare for *to be seasick*

Idioms

Acqua in bocca! For *Mom's word*

Affogare in un bicchier d'acqua for *to be overwhelmed by small problems* (literally: to drown in a glass of water)

Andare a gonfie vele for *things are going very well* (literally: at full sail)

Andare a letto con le galline for *to go to bed early* (literally: to go to bed with the hens)

Andare d'accordo for *to get along*

Avere gli occhi più grandi dello stomaco for *to want more than you need* (literally: to have eyes bigger than the stomach)

Avere la testa tra le nuvole for *not to be thinking* (literally: to have your head in the clouds)

Avere le braccine corte for *to be cheap* (literally: to have short arms)

Avere le mani in pasta for *to have the finger in the pie* (literally: to have your hands in the dough)

Avere sale in zucca for *to be smart* (literally: to have salt in the pumpkin, i.e., your head)

Avere un diavolo per capello for *to be as mad as hell* (literally: to have a demon on each hair)

Avere una gatta da pelare for *to have a big problem* (literally: to have a cat to peel)

Avere uno scheletro nell'armadio for *to have a secret* (literally: to have a skeleton in the closet)

Avere uno stomaco di ferro for *to have an iron-cast stomach*

Bello come il sole for *beautiful like the sun*

Bere come una spugna for *to drink like a fish* (literally: to drink like a sponge)

Brutto come la fame for *ugly like hunger*

Buono come il pane for *goodhearted*

Cadere dalla padella nella brace for *to go from a bad situation to a worse one* (literally: to go from the pan into the embers)

Cadere dalle nuvole for *taken aback* (literally: to fall from the clouds)

Cambiare le carte in tavola for *taking back what you said* (literally: to change the cards on the table)

Capire al volo for *to catch on immediately*

Capitare a fagiolo for *perfect timing* (literally: to happen at the bean)

Cavolo! For *darn!* (literally: cauliflower!)

Cercare il pelo nell'uovo for *to be picky* (literally: to look for the hair in the egg)

Cercare un ago in un pagliaio for *to find a needle in a haystack*

Cogliere un'occasione al volo for *to jump at the opportunity* (literally: to catch a flying opportunity)

Conosco i miei polli for *to be aware of the personality of your friends/colleagues/...* (literally: to know your own chickens)

Dalle stelle alle stalle for *to go from a great situation to the worst* (literally: from the stars to the stables)

Darsi la zappa sui piedi for *to put one's foot in one's mouth*

Dire pane al pane e vino al vino for *let's call a spade a spade*

Dormire (o riposare) sugli allori for *to rest on one's laurel*

Dormire come un ghiro for *sleep like a dog*

Dormire tra due guanciali for *to feel safe* (literally: to sleep between two pillows)

È inutile piangere sul latte versato for *it is no use crying over spilled milk*

Essere al verde for *to have no money/to be broke*

Essere in un bel pasticcio for *to be in a pickle*

Essere nella stessa barca for *to be in the same situation* (literally: to be in the same boat)

Fa un freddo cane for *it is freezing cold*

Fare ad occhio e croce for *to act on the back of a gross evaluation*

Fare i conti in tasca for *to pry into someone's financial situation*

Fare i conti senza l'oste for *to make a decision without consulting the person in charge*

Fare l'avvocato del diavolo for *playing the Devil's advocate*

Fare la nanna for *to sleep*

Fare la pelle for *to kill*

Farsi in quattro for *to bend over backward*

Gettare fumo negli occhi for *to trick somebody* (literally: to throw smoke in the eyes)

Gettare il guanto for *to challenge* (literally: to throw the glove)

Imbrogliare una matassa for *to make things more complicated*

In bocca al lupo! for *good luck!*

In tempo di tempesta ogni buco è un porto for *any port in a storm*

Ingoiare il rospo for *to eat crow* (literally: to swallow the toad)

Lasciare la bocca amara for *to be left disappointed* (literally: to leave the mouth bitter)

Lavare la testa a qualcuno for *to severely scold somebody* (literally: to wash somebody's head)

Legarsela al dito for *to never forget [something negative]* (literally: to tie it around the finger)

Levare le tende for *to go wary* (literally: to remove the tents)

Lupo di mare for *old salt, sea dog* (literally: sea wolf)

Mandare avanti la barca for *to keep going in hard times* (literally: send the boat forward)

Marinaio della domenica for *Sunday or fair-weather sailor*

Mettere il carro innanzi ai buoi for *to do something before being ready* (literally: to put the cart before the oxen)

Morire dalla voglia for *to looking forward to something* (literally: to die from the longing)

Nascere con la camicia for *to be very lucky* (literally: to be born with a button-down shirt)

Nascondersi dietro un dito for *to deny everything* (literally: to hide behind a finger)

Navigare su internet for *to surf/search the web*

Non avere peli sulla lingua for *to speak frankly* (literally to have no hairs on the tongue)

Non mi rompere le scatole for *stop annoying me* (literally: do not break the balls)

Non poterne più for *not being able to stand something any longer*

Non sapere che pesci pigliare for *not to know how to behave or how to react* (literally: not to know which fish to catch)

Non vedere l'ora for *not able to wait for something* (literally: to not be able to see the time)

Oltre al danno anche la beffa for *to add insult to injury*

Pagare alla romana for *to Dutch* (literally: to go the Roman way)

Passarne di tutti i colori for *to go through all sorts of problems* (literally: to go through all colors)

Pescare qualcuno con le mani nel sacco for *to catch someone in the act* (literally: to fish someone with their hands in the sack)

Pesci in faccia for *to treat like dirt* (literally: fish in the face)

Prendere due piccioni con una fava for *to solve two problems with one solution* (literally: to catch two pigeons with one stone)

Prendere in giro for *to pull someone's leg* (literally: to take around)

Prendere lucciole per lanterne for *to misunderstand completely* (literally: to take firefly for lanterns)

Prendere un granchio for *to make a mistake* (literally: to catch a crab)

Promettere mari e monti for *to promise more than you can deliver* (literally: to promise seas and mountains)

Qualcosa bolle in pentola for *what's cooking* (literally: something boils in the pan)

Ride bene chi ride ultimo for *he who laughs last, laughs longer*

Rompere il ghiaccio for *to start a conversation* (literally: to break the ice)

Sano come un pesce for *perfectly healthy* (literally: healthy as a fish)

Saperne una più del diavolo for *to be up to more tricks than Old Nick* (literally: to know one more than the Devil)

Scoprire l'acqua calda for *to discover the wheel* (literally: to discover the warm water)

Senz'altro for *certainly*

Sogni d'oro! for *sweet dreams!*

Sputare il rospo for *to blurt out* (literally: to spit the toad)

Sputare nel piatto dove mangi for *to bite the hand that feeds you* (literally: to spit on the plate that feeds you)

Stare con le mani in mano for *to twiddle one's thumb* (literally: to stay with your hands in hand)

Tagliare i ponti for *to cut all communication* (literally: to cut the bridges)

Tenere le dita incrociate for *to keep one's fingers crossed*

Tirare i remi in barca for *to back down, give something a rest* (literally: pull the oars into the boat)

Scoprire l'America for *to find the pot of gold at the end of the rainbow* (literally: to find the Americas)

Tutto fa brodo for *all is grist for the mill* (literally: anything goes)

Un coniglio for *a scaredy cat* (literally: a rabbit)

Un pezzo di pane for *a good egg*

Un pezzo grosso for *a big shot*

Un'oca giuliva for *a silly* (female) *person* (literally: a happy goose)

Una civetta for *a flirty woman* (literally: an owl)

Una persona in gamba for *a very able person*

Una volpe for *a street-smart person* (literally: a fox)

Vai a quel paese for *get lost!*

Valere la pena for *to be worth it*

Voler cavar sangue da una rapa for *to get blood out of a stone* (literally: to want to get blood out of a turnip)

Proverbs

Proverbs are still a big part of the culture and are considered a great source of *folk wisdom* (***saggezza popolare***). They are still mentioned and used in everyday language to the point that often it is only necessary to mention just the first half of one to be understood:

> ***A buon intenditor, poche parole*** for *few words to the wise* (literally: to the good listener, few words)

A caval donato non si guarda in bocca for *be grateful for the gift without checking its value* (literally: don't look a gift horse in the mouth)

A goccia a goccia si scava la roccia for *little by little you can overcome the most difficult obstacles* (literally: drop after drop you dig the rock)

A mali estremi, estremi rimedi for *in extremely bad situations you need to use extreme remedies* (literally: desperate times call for desperate measures)

Acqua cheta rompe i ponti for *do not underestimate quiet people because they might reveal dangerous things* (literally: the quiet water breaks the bridges)

Ad ognuno la sua croce for *everyone has his own problems* (literally: to each one his own crucifix)

Aiutati che Dio t'aiuta for *God helps those who help themselves* (literally: help yourself, for God helps you)

Al cuore non si comanda for *you cannot decide who or what to love* (literally: the heart can not be ruled)

Ambasciator non porta pena for *who delivers the bad news has no responsibility for them* (literally: the ambassador does not bring the pain).

Anche l'occhio vuole la sua parte for *appearances are important too* (literally: also the eye wants its share)

Batti il ferro quando è caldo for *strike while the iron is hot* (literally: beat the iron while it is hot)

Buon sangue non mente for *the apple does not fall far from the tree* (literally: good blood does not lie)

Campa cavallo che l'erba cresce for *to comment on empty promises or unfavorable and unlikely situations, like when a horse has to wait for the grass to grow to be able to eat* (literally: live horse that the grass grows)

Can che abbaia non morde for *barking dogs never bite* (literally: a dog that barks does not bite)

Cento teste, cento cappelli for *you will have as many different points of view or wishes as many people have* (literally: a hundred heads, a hundred hats)

Chi ben comincia è a metà dell'opera for *getting started is already like having done half of the work* or *well begun is half done* (literally: who starts well has done half of the job)

Chi cerca, trova for *only who looks for things can find them* (literally: who searches, finds)

Chi di spada ferisce di spada perisce for *one who uses violence can expect a violent response* (literally: who inflicts wounds with a sword will die because of a sword)

Chi dice donna dice danno for *women mean trouble* (literally: who says woman says damage)

Chi disprezza compra for *usually you complain about things that you actually like* (literally: who despises, buys)

Chi dorme non piglia pesci for *you need to act to be productive* or *you snooze, you lose* (literally: who sleeps does not catch fish)

Chi è causa del suo mal pianga se stesso for *who is the cause of his troubles can only blame himself* (literally: whom is the source of his pain has to cry for himself)

Chi è senza peccato scagli la prima pietra for *you need not have committed any mistake to be able to blame somebody for his* (literally: whoever is without sin, cast the first stone)

Chi fa da sé fa per tre for *sometimes you do better without anybody's help* (literally: who works by himself does the work of three people)

Chi ha avuto ha avuto e chi ha dato ha dato for *to put an end to a dispute regardless of what has been gained or lost* (literally: who have taken, have taken, and who have given, have given)

Chi ha i denti non ha pane, e chi ha pane non ha i denti for *you either have the ability to appreciate things or you have things, but do not appreciate what you have* (literally: who has teeth does not have bread and who has bread does not have teeth)

Chi ha tempo non aspetti tempo for *do not waste your time* (literally: who has time, should not wait)

Chi la dura la vince for *keep going* (literally: the one who lasts, wins)

Chi la fa l'aspetti for *what goes around comes around* (literally: who commits [something], should expect [to receive] the same thing)

Chi lascia la strada vecchia per la nuova, sa quel che lascia ma non sa quel che trova for *do not leave what is known and safe for something unknown and risky* (literally: who leaves the old road for the new one, knows what he's leaving, but does not know what he will find)

Chi nasce tondo non può morir quadrato for *you cannot change the kind of character you were born with* (literally: who was born round can not die a square)

Chi non beve in compagnia o è un ladro o è una spia for *you should participate in the fun of the party unless you have something to hide* (literally: who does not drink with the rest of the party is either a thief or a spy)

Chi non muore si rivede for *long time no see* (literally: those who do not die see each other again)

Chi non risica non rosica for *if you do not take chances, you do not gain anything* (literally: nothing ventured nothing gained).

Chi rompe paga e i cocci sono i suoi for *any damage must be paid for* (literally: who breaks, pays and keeps the pieces)

Chi sa fa e chi non sa insegna for *distrust who gives unsolicited advice* (literally: who knows, acts, and who does not know, teaches)

Chi semina raccoglie for *you reap what you saw*

Chi semina vento raccoglie tempesta for *bad actions have worse consequences* (literally: who reaps wind, harvests storm)

Chi si accontenta gode for *if you are happy with what you have, you will relish it* (literally: who settles, enjoys)

Chi si loda si imbroda for *self-praise can damage* (literally: who self-praises, makes a mess for himself)

Chi si scusa si accusa for *if you apologize you accuse yourself* (literally: he who excuses himself, accuses himself)

Chi si somiglia si piglia for *people who look alike often become a couple* (literally: who resemble each other, take each other)

Chi tace acconsente for *you agree if you do not speak up* (literally: who keeps quiet, agrees)

Chi tardi arriva male alloggia for *the last to arrive will have the worst accommodation* (literally: who arrives late, stays badly)

Chi troppo e chi niente for *the wealth is distributed unfairly* (literally: who [has] too much and who [has] nothing)

Chi troppo vuole nulla stringe for *who tries to get too much may end up with nothing* (literally: who wants too much, grips nothing)

Chi trova un amico trova un tesoro for *friends are the most precious thing* (literally: who finds a friend, find a treasure)

Chi va con lo zoppo, impara a zoppicare for *you take the bad habits of the people you spend time with* (literally: who goes with the lame learns how to limp)

Chi va piano va sano e va lontano for *it is better to go slowly rather than to be in a rush* (literally: who goes slowly goes healthy and far)

Chi vivrà vedrà for *only the future can tell who was right* (literally: who will live, will see)

Chiodo scaccia chiodo for *a new problem takes away an old problem* (literally: a nail drives away a nail)

Con le buone maniere si ottiene tutto for *always be polite* (literally: with good manners, you can obtain anything)

Da cosa nasce cosa for *one thing leads to another* (literally: form one thing, another is born)

Dagli amici mi guardi Iddio che dai nemici mi guardo io for *we are open to the bad actions of our friends because we are busy guarding against our enemies* (literally: God protects me from my friends because I am guarding against my enemies)

Del senno di poi sono piene le fosse for *it is easy to understand after the fact* (literally: the graves are full of hindsight)

Di necessità si fa virtù for *to make a virtue out of necessity*

Dimmi con chi vai, e ti dirò chi sei for *to understand what kind of person somebody is you need to look at who she/he* *spends time with* (literally: tell me who you go with and I will tell who you are)

Dio li fa e poi li accoppia for *similar people often become a couple* (literally: God makes them and then pairs them)

Domandare è lecito, rispondere è cortesia for *when somebody does not want to answer your question even when it was predictable* (literally: to ask is legitimate; to answer is kindness)

Due torti non fanno una ragione for *two wrongs do not make one right*

È inutile piangere sul latte versato for *there is no point crying over spilled milk*

È meglio essere uccel di bosco, che uccel di gabbia for *it is better to be free and wild than caged in safety* (literally: it is better to be a bird of the woods than a bird in a cage)

Fare buon viso a cattivo gioco for *you need to adapt in unfavorable circumstances* (literally: it is necessary to put on a nice face in a bad game)

Fare il passo più lungo della gamba for *to overestimate the ability to deal with a situation* (literally: to make a step longer than the leg)

Fatta la legge, trovato l'inganno for *there is always somebody who will try not to obey it* (literally: made the law, found the loophole)

Fidarsi è bene, non fidarsi è meglio for *it is always better to be cautious* (literally: to trust is good, not to trust is better)

Figlio troppo accarezzato non fu mai bene allevato for *a spoiled child is not a well raised child* (literally: a too caressed son has never been a too well raised child)

Finché c'è vita c'è speranza for *never lose hope* (literally: as long as there is life there is hope)

Fortunato al gioco, sfortunato in amore for *when you are lucky with gambling you are not lucky in love* (literally: lucky at cards, unlucky with love)

Gallina vecchia fa buon brodo for *experience counts as in the case of an old person* (literally: an old hen makes a good broth)

Grande amore, gran dolore for *a great love [is followed by] a great sorrow*

I panni sporchi si lavano in famiglia for *family secrets can only be shared within the family* (literally: the dirty laundry is washed in the family)

I parenti sono come le scarpe, più sono stretti, più fanno male for *the closest the relatives the more the problems* (literally: relatives are like shoes: the tighter, the more painful)

Il buon giorno si vede dal mattino for *something that start well, will go well* (literally: a good day can be seen by the morning)

Il denaro fa l'uomo ricco! L'educazione lo fa signore for *education will give you nobility/class not money* (literally: money makes a man rich! Education makes it a gentleman)

Il gioco è bello quando dura poco for *even a beautiful thing can become a bore* (literally: the game is good when it is short)

Il gioco non vale la candela for *something is not worth the effort* (literally: the game is not worth the candle)

Il lupo perde il pelo ma non il vizio for *it is difficult to lose bad habits* (literally: the wolf loses the fur, but not the vice)

Il mondo è fatto a scale, c'è chi scende e c'è chi sale for *good luck sometimes favors others* (literally: the world is made of stairs; some go down and some go up)

Il riso abbonda sulla bocca degli stolti for *laughing too much is a sign of stupidity* (literally: laughing is plentiful on the mouth of the uneducated)

Il silenzio è d'oro for *silence is gold*

Impara l'arte e mettila da parte for *learning a new skill is always useful even when you do not need to use it immediately* (literally: learn the art and put it aside)

L'abito non fa il monaco for *clothes do not make the man*

L'amore non è bello se non è litigarello for *a relationship is alive when two people frequently confront each other on small things* (literally: love is not beautiful if there is no arguing)

L'appetito vien mangiando for *the more you have, the more you want* (literally: the appetite comes with eating)

L'erba cattiva non muore mai for *bad people always survive* (literally: the bad grass never dies)

L'erba del vicino è sempre più verde for *what other people own always seem more valuable* (literally: the grass of the neighbor is always greener)

L'occasione fa l'uomo ladro for *the opportunity makes the thief*

L'ospite è come il pesce: dopo tre giorni puzza for *short visits are better* (literally: the guest is like fish: after three days starts smelling)

L'ozio è il padre di tutti i vizi for *lazy people are more likely to acquire more vices* (literally: idleness is the father of all the vices)

La fortuna aiuta gli audaci for *fortune favors the bold*

La lingua batte dove il dente duole for *you always end up talking about the most painful topics* (literally: the tongue ever turns to the aching tooth)

La madre degli imbecilli è sempre incinta for *the world will always be full of imbeciles* (literally: the mother of imbeciles is always pregnant)

La miglior difesa è l'attacco for *offense is the best defense*

La via dell'Inferno è lastricata di buone intenzioni for *the road to hell is paved with good intentions*

Le bugie hanno le gambe corte for *lies get quickly uncovered* (literally: lies have short legs)

Le disgrazie non vengono mai sole for *there is never just one problem at the time* (literally: adversities never come alone)

Le vie del Signore sono infinite for *solutions to problems often appear in unexpected ways* (literally: the paths of God are infinite)

Lontano dagli occhi, lontano dal cuore for *feelings will dissipate with time* (literally: far from the eyes, far from the heart)

Mal comune mezzo gaudio for *sharing misfortune helps to deal with it* (literally: shared misfortune, half a joy)

Meglio soli che male accompagnati for *you should always be choosy about the people you spend time with* (literally: better alone than in bad company)

Meglio tardi che mai for *better late than never*

Morto un papa se ne fa un altro for *nobody is irreplaceable* (literally: when one pope is dead, a new one is made)

Natale con i tuoi, Pasqua con chi vuoi for *tradition wants you with your family for Christmas and with whoever you choose for Easter* (literally: Christmas with yours, Easter with who you want)

Ne uccide più la lingua che la spada for *words hurt more than actions* (literally: the tongue kills more than the sword)

Nella botte piccola c'è il vino buono for *do not disregard small things* (literally: the good wine is in the small barrel)

Non c'è peggior sordo di chi non vuol sentire for *it is useless to talk to somebody who does not want to listen* (literally: there is nothing duller than those who do not want to hear)

Non dire gatto se non ce l'hai nel sacco for *do not take for granted an accomplishment* (literally: do not say cat if he is not in the sack)

Non è bello ciò che è bello, ma è bello ciò che piace for *different people have different taste* (literally: it is not beautiful what is beautiful, but it is beautiful what you like)

Non è tutto oro quel che luccica for *beautiful things may not be the best things* (literally: not all that sparkles is gold)

Non fasciarti la testa prima di rompertela for *do not worry before there is any need for worrying* (literally: do not wrap your head before it is broken)

Non si può avere la botte piena e la moglie ubriaca for *you cannot have your cake and eat it too*

Non svegliar il can che dorme for *do not instigate a relaxed but dangerous person* (literally: do not wake the sleeping dog)

Non tutte le ciambelle escono con il buco for *not every project is realized perfectly* (literally: not every doughnut comes out with a hole)

Non tutto il male vien per nuocere for *sometimes there is a positive side to misfortune* (literally: not all evil comes to harm)

Occhio non vede, cuore non duole for *what you do not know does not hurt you* (literally: eye does not see, heart does not ache)

Oggi a me domani a te for *nobody is immune to misfortune* (literally: today to you, tomorrow to me)

Ogni lasciata è persa for *take your chances* (literally: every [opportunity that] we let go is [a] lost [opportunity]).

Ogni promessa è debito for *you need to keep your word* (literally: every promise is a debt)

Ognuno tira l'acqua al proprio mulino for *every man to himself* (literally: everyone pulls the water to his mill)

Paese che vai usanza che trovi for *you need to be open to different things* (literally: country where you go, customs that you find)

Patti chiari amicizia lunga for *if the agreement is clear there is no reason for arguing* (literally: clear agreement, long friendship)

Piove sempre sul bagnato for *when it rains it pours* (literally: it always rains on the wetness)

Quando c'è la salute c'è tutto for *health is the most important thing* (literally: when there is health there is everything)

Quando il gatto non c'è i topi ballano for *without any control everybody is up to something* (literally: when the cat is not there, the mice dance)

Quando la volpe non arriva all'uva dice che è acerba for *we scorn what we cannot achieve* (literally: when the fox cannot reach the grapes, it says they are not ripe)

Quando si chiude una porta si apre un portone for *when an opportunity disappears, a bigger one will present* (literally: when a door closes, a front door opens)

Quando si è in ballo bisogna ballare for *you need to finish what you started* (literally: when you are at the dance you need to dance)

Roma non fu fatta in un giorno for *you need time [and patience] to build something* (literally: Rome was not built in one day)

Rosso di sera, bel tempo si spera for *when the sky is red at sunset, there is reasonable chance of good weather the following day* (literally: red in the evening, good weather is hoped for)

Sbagliando si impara for *you learn from your mistakes*

Se non è zuppa è pan bagnato for *six of one, half a dozen of the other* (literally: if it is not soup it's soaked bread)

Se son rose fioriranno for *the situation will develop as it is destined* (literally: if there are roses, they will bloom)

Si dice il peccato, ma non il peccatore for *there is no need to reveal who committed the deed* (literally: you tell the sin, not the sinner)

Soli non si starebbe bene nemmeno in Paradiso for *loneliness is the worst feeling* (literally: even in Heaven it would not feel good to be alone)

Tanto fumo e poco arrosto for *all talk and no action* (literally: a lot of smoke, and no roast)

Tanto va la gatta al lardo che ci lascia lo zampino for *curiosity killed the cat* (literally: the (female) cat goes so often to the lard that she leaves her pawprints there)

Tentar non nuoce for *you need to at least try* (literally: trying does not hurt)

Tira più un capello di donna che cento paia di buoi for *women are the most powerful* (literally: a hair of a woman can pull more than what one hundred pairs of oxen can)

Tra i due litiganti il terzo gode for *between the two parties, the third gains*

Tra il dire e il fare c'è di mezzo il mare for *there is a big discrepancy between our words and our actions* (literally: between saying and doing there is the sea)

Tra moglie e marito non mettere il dito for *it is better not to intrude in a family matter* (literally: between wife and husband do not put your finger)

Troppi cuochi rovinano il brodo for *when many people do something together they need to coordinate to avoid disaster* (literally: too many cooks spoil the broth)

Tutte le strade portano a Roma for *different strategies take you to the same solution* (literally: all roads lead to Rome)

Tutti i nodi vengono al pettine for *at some point we will have to face our mistakes or challenges* (literally: all the knots come to the comb)

Tutto il mondo è paese for *you find the same kind of problems everywhere* (literally: all the world is a village)

Una ciliegia tira l'altra for *one thing leads to another* (literally: one cherry pulls another)

Una mano lava l'altra e tutte e due lavano il viso for *collaboration is important* (literally: one hand washes the other, and together they wash the face)

Una mela al giorno leva il medico di torno for *an apple a day keeps the doctor away*

Una rondine non fa primavera for *it is better not to draw fast conclusions* (literally: one swallow does not make spring)

Uomo avvisato mezzo salvato for *forewarned is forearmed* (Literally: a warned man is a half-saved man)

Vale più la pratica che la grammatica for *experience is more important than theory* (literally: practice is worth more than grammar)

Vivi e lascia vivere for *live and let live*

Chapter 9 - Essential Grammar

Throughout the book, "grammar tips" were placed where could they be useful. Here they all are, and some more, to be consulted when needed.

Nouns, Articles, Adjectives, and Pronouns

Italian nouns have both natural and grammatical gender: they are either feminine or masculine. Natural gender comes from the meaning of the noun: whether it is a boy or girl. Grammatical gender is arbitrary and needs to be learned. It is important to know since articles, adjectives, and pronouns have to agree (be of the same gender) with the nouns they go with or stand for (in the case of the pronoun). The gender is often identified by the last vowel and usually is *-o* for masculine and *-a* for feminine:

Il ragazzo è bello for *the boy is handsome*

La ragazza è bella for *the girl is beautiful*

Lui è bello for *he is handsome*

Lei è bella for *she is beautiful*

Il gatto è rosso for *the* [male] *cat* [male] *is red* [male]

La gatta è rossa for *the* [female] *cat* [female] *is red* [female]

Lui è rosso for *he is red* [male]

Lei è rossa for *she is red* [female]

Il treno è nuovo for *the train is new* [male]

La macchina è nuova for *the car is new* [female]

Sometimes, things are a bit harder, such as: exceptions, regularities, patterns, and professions.

Nouns ending in *-e* can be either feminine (*la canzone*/*the song*, *la chiave*/*the key*, *la classe*/*the class*, *la lezione*/*the lesson*, *la nave*/*the ship*, *la notte*/*the night*) or masculine (*il fiore*/*flower*, *il giornale*/*the newspaper*, *il mare*/ *the sea*, *il pane*/*the bread*, *il sale*/*the salt*, *il cane*/*the dog*) without a way of predicting it.

Few high-frequency feminine nouns end in *-o*: *mano* (*hand*), *foto* (*picture, photo*), *auto* (*car*), and *radio* (*radio*).

There are some regularities that help predict when a noun ending in -*a* or *-e* is masculine (like for endings such as *-amma, -ima, -ema, -ale, -ame, -ile, one, -ore*): *il dramma* (*the drama*), *il programma* (*the program*), *il clima* (*the climate*), *il dilemma* (*the dilemma*), *il sistema* (*the system*), *l'animale* (*the animal*), *il bastone* (*the cane*), *il catrame* (*the tar*), *il dottore* (*the doctor*), *il porcile* (*the pig pen*).

Regularities also help identify noun endings in *-e* as feminine (as for endings like *-sione, -zione* or *-si*): *la pensione* (*the pension*), *la stazione* (*the station*), *l'illusione* (*the illusion*), *l'ipotesi* (*the hypothesis*), *l'analisi* (*the analysis*), *la crisi* (*the crisis*).

Patterns may determine whether a word is masculine or feminine, like in the case of a fruit (generally feminine) and its tree (generally masculine). Fruits: *arancia* (*orange* – feminine), *ciliegia* (*cherry* – feminine), *mela* (*apple* – feminine), *pera* (*pear* – feminine), *pesca* (*peach* – feminine). Trees: *arancio* (*orange tree* – masculine), *ciliegio* (*cherry tree* – masculine), *melo* (*apple tree* – masculine), *pero* (*pear tree* –masculine), *pesco* (*peach tree* – masculine).

When speaking about people and their professions, there are different endings for men and women.

When the masculine ending is *-tore*, the feminine ending is *-trice*:

attore and *attrice* (*actor* and *actress*), *pittore* and *pittrice* (*painter*, masculine and feminine), *scrittore* and *scrittrice* (*writer* masculine and feminine), *scultore* and *scultrice* (*sculptor* and *sculptress*).

When the masculine ends in *-ore* the feminine ends in *-oressa*:

Dottore and *dottoressa* (*doctor* – male and female), *professore* and *professoressa* (*professor* – male and female).

For professions ending in *–ista*, the gender of the person is revealed by the article: *il dentista* (*the* [male] *dentist*) and *la dentista* (*the* [female] *dentist*), *il pianista* (*the* [male] *pianist*) and *la pianista* (*the* [female] *pianist*).

Last, like in English, plural nouns are different from their singular form. In English, most of the time an *-s* is added at the end of the word; in Italian, the final vowel changes in a regular manner.

Singular words ending with *-o* and *-e* have their plural counterpart ending in *-i:*

ragazzo (*boy*) and *ragazzi* (*boys*)

vino (*wine*) and *vini* (*wines*)

libro (*book*) and *libri* (*books*)

Amico (*friend*) and *amici* (*friends*)

Chiave (*key*) and *chiavi* (*keys*)

Fiume (*river*) and *fiumi* (*rivers*)

Padre (*father*) and *padri* (*fathers*)

Giornale (*newspaper*) and *giornali* (*newspapers*)

Singular nouns that end in *-a* change their ending to *-e* in their plural form:

Lettera (*letter*) and *lettere* (*letters*)

Statua (*statue*) and *statue* (*statues*)

Sorella (*sister*) and *sorelle* (*sisters*)

Strada (*street*) and *strade* (*streets*)

Few words do not change in their plural version, only their article does. Singular words ending in -i (*ipotesi*/*hypothesis*, *crisi*/*crisis*, *analisi*/*analysis* and *tesi*/*thesis*) mark their plural with the plural article (*le ipotesi*/*the hypothesis*, *le crisi*/*the crisis*, *le analisi*/*the analyses*, *le tesi*/*the thesis*). Few nouns end in a consonant rather than a vowel and they also mark their plural with the article (*il film*/*the movie* and *i film*/*the movies*, *lo smog*/*the smog* and *gli smog*/*the smogs*, *lo sport*/*the sport* and *gli sport*/*the sports*).

Articles

As you already might have noticed, Italian definitive articles are quite relevant and need to agree with the nouns they precede. It is quite straightforward: *la* is the feminine singular and becomes *le* in its plural form; *il* and *lo* are the used for the singular masculine nouns and turn respectively in *i* and *gli*. As a general rule, when the article ends with a vowel (*la*, *le*, *lo*), and the noun starts with a vowel, then the article drops its vowel and this process is marked by an apostrophe in the orthography: *la amica* (*the friend* [female]) becomes *l'amica*.

Italian indefinite articles correspond to the English *a, an,* and *some. Un* is the indefinite article for masculine nouns and *z, s*+consonant, *ps* or *gn*. Uno and *un* precede masculine nouns, and *una* precedes feminine nouns and becomes *un'* when the noun starts with a vowel.

Un aeroplano for *an airplane*

Un cane for *a dog*

Un panino for *a sandwich*

Uno gnomo for *a gnome*

Uno psicologo for *a psychologist*

Uno scrittore for *a writer*

Uno stadio for *a stadium*

Uno zaino for *a backpack*

Una donna for *a woman*

Una stazione for *a station*

Un'automobile for *a car*

Adjectives

Adjectives modify nouns, or specify them, <u>describing</u> them; they need to agree with the gender and number of the noun they refer to, changing their ending accordingly, and they usually follow the noun:

Il gatto nero for *the black cat* or *i gatti neri* for *the black cats*

La donna alta for *the tall woman* or *le donne alte* for *the tall women*

Adjectives ending in *-e* can describe both masculine and feminine nouns and become *-i* for the plural:

Il prato verde for *the green lawn* or *i prati verdi* for *the green lawns*

Il libro interessante for *the interesting book* or *i libri interessanti* for *the interesting books*

Il pacco pesante for *the heavy package* or *i pacchi pesanti* for *the heavy packages*

A particular set of descriptive adjectives are those referring to nationalities; they follow the same rules as the other adjectives and are <u>not</u> capitalized:

La signora italiana, tedesca, francese for *the Italian, German, French lady*

Le signore italiane, tedesche, francesi for *the Italian, German, French ladies*

Il signore italiano, tedesco, francese for *the Italian, German, French gentleman*

I signori italiani, tedeschi, francesi for *the Italian, German, French gentlemen*

Essential adjectives:

Bello for *beautiful, handsome* becomes *belli* (plural), *bella* (feminine singular), *belle* (feminine plural)

Buono for good becomes *buoni* (plural), *buona* (feminine singular), *buone* (feminine plural)

Bravo for able becomes *bravi* (plural), *brava* (feminine singular), *brave* (feminine plural)

Brutto for ugly becomes *brutti* (plural), *brutta* (feminine singular), *brutte* (feminine plural)

Caro for dear becomes *cari* (plural), *cara* (feminine singular), *care* (feminine plural)

Cattivo for bad becomes *cattivi* (plural), *cattiva* (feminine singular), *cattive* (feminine plural)

Giovane for young (singular feminine and masculine) becomes *giovani* (plural feminine and masculine)

Grande for big (singular feminine and masculine) becomes *grandi* (plural feminine and masculine)

Lungo for *long* becomes *lunghi* (plural), *lunga* (feminine singular), *lunghe* (feminine plural)

Nuovo for *new* becomes *nuovi* (plural), *nuova* (feminine singular), *nuove* (feminine plural)

Piccolo for *little*, small becomes *piccoli* (plural), *piccola* (feminine singular), *piccole* (feminine plural)

Vecchio for *old* becomes *vecchi* (plural), *vecchia* (feminine singular), *vecchie* (feminine plural)

Molto for *much* becomes *molti* (plural: *many*), *molta* (feminine singular), *molte* (feminine plural)

Poco for a *little* becomes *pochi* (plural: *a few*), *poca* (feminine singular), *poche* (feminine plural)

Tutto for *all* becomes *tutti* (plural: *every*), *tutta* (feminine singular), *tutte* (feminine plural)

Altro for *other*, *another* becomes *altri* (plural), *altra* (feminine singular), *altre* (feminine plural)

Prossimo for *next* becomes *prossimi* (plural), *prossima* (feminine singular), *prossime* (feminine plural)

Ultimo for *last* becomes *ultimi* (plural), *ultima* (feminine singular), *ultime* (feminine plural)

Key adjectives:

Arancione for *orange*

Azzurro for *light blue*

Bianco for *white*

Blu for *dark blue*

Giallo for *yellow*

Grigio for *gray*

Marrone for *brown*

Nero for *black*

Rosso for *red*

Rosa for *pink*

Verde for *green*

Viola for *purple*

Allegro for *happy*

Avaro for *stingy*

Brutto for *ugly*

Bugiardo for *liar*

Caldo for *warm*

Carino for *nice*

Caro for *expensive*

Debole for *weak*

Delizioso for *delicious*

Difficile for *difficult*

Disgustoso for *disgusting*

Facile for *easy*

Fantastico for *fantastic*

Freddo for *cold*

Generoso for *generous*

Giovane for *young*

Grande for *big*

Grasso for *fat*

Indipendente for *independent*

Magro for *thin*

Meraviglioso for *wonderful*

Piccolo for *small*

Povero for *poor*

Profumato for *fragrant*

Pulito for *clean*

Ricco for *rich*

Sincero for *sincere*

Sporco for *dirty*

Possessive adjectives

Adjectives that precede the nouns can indicate possession (possessive), or indicate which object or person you are referring to (demonstratives), or indicate inner properties (***bello****/beautiful,* ***buono****/good,* ***generoso****/generous*), quantities (***molti****/many,* ***pochi****/few*), timing (***prossimo****/next,* ***ultimo****/last*):

Il mio libro, i miei libri for *my book, my books*

La mia casa, le mie case for *my house, my houses*

Il tuo giornale, i tuoi giornali for *my newspaper, my newspapers*

La tua macchina, le tue macchine for *your car, your cars*

Il suo viaggio, i suoi viaggi for *his trip, his trips*

La sua storia, le sue storie for *her story, her stories*

Il nostro divano, i nostri divani for *our couch, our couches*

La nostra vacanza, le nostre vacanze for *our vacation, our vacations*

Il vostro tavolo, i vostri tavoli for *your table, your tables*

La vostra sedia, le vostre sedie for *your chair, your chairs*

Il loro orologio, i loro orologi for *their watch, their watches*

La loro pianta, le loro piante for *their plant, their plants*

Demonstrative adjectives

Demonstrative adjectives are used to indicate a specific person or object; hence, they agree in number and gender with the noun they refer to:

Questo, questa for *this* (masculine and feminine respectively)

Questi, queste for *these* (masculine and feminine respectively)

Quello, quella for *that* (masculine and feminine respectively)

Quelli, quelle for *those* (masculine and feminine respectively)

Questo ragazzo è intelligente for *this boy is smart*

Questa signora è molto elegante for *this lady is very elegant*

Ho comprato questi orologi for *I bought these watches*

Ho tagliato queste mele for *I cut these apples*

Quelle ragazze sono molto felici for *those girls are very happy*

Comparatives and superlatives

Comparatives express *"more... than"* (*più... che/del*), *"less... than"* (*"meno... che/del"*), the same as *(così come, tanti quanti*) and they are used very similarly in English and Italian:

Ci sono più cani che gatti for *there are more dogs than cats*

La rivista è meno interessante del libro for *the magazine is less interesting than the book*

Roma è tanto bella quanto caotica for *Rome is as beautiful as chaotic*

Superlatives indicate the most or the least and they are expressed as in English by *the most* (*il più*) or *the least* (*il meno*): *la donna più ricca del mondo* for *the richest woman in the world*

The absolute superlative in English is rendered by *very/most* or the ending *-est* and in Italian by *molto* and the ending *-issimo*: *Il film è molto bello* for *the movie is very good* or *l'inverno è freddissimo* for *the winter is very cold.*

Pronouns

In Italian, there are at least eight possible personal pronouns that function as a subject, while in English, there are only six. The main difference is that, in English, *you* is used to either indicate one or many people different from yourself; in Italian, you will say either *tu* if it is only one person or *voi* if you refer to many people. The feminine version of the third person (*lei*) is also used as the formal version for *you* for either a lady or a gentleman: when you meet someone for the first time, when you do not have a personal relationship with someone, and when somebody is older than you. Often, when used as a formal version of *tu*, Lei is written with a capital letter, even when at the end of words like in *ho deciso di scriverLe* (*I decided to write to you*). However, this practice is falling into disuse.

As you have seen in the previous chapters, and you will see in the section dedicated to the verbs, a peculiarity of Italian is that you do not really need to mention the subject (or the pronoun that stands for it) unless you want to—since the inflection of the verb gives away who is performing the action.

Io (only capitalized at the beginning of a sentence) for *I*

Tu for *you*

Lei for *she*

Lui for *he*

Noi for *we*

Voi for *you* (many)

Loro or *essi* for *they*

Direct object pronouns

Pronouns can be used as a direct object (i.e., *me, him, us...*) instead of a noun to show who or what is affected by the action of the verb. Like in *I like her a lot, I admire him immensely, I saw them yesterday*. In Italian, there is a set of direct object pronouns, and they can be either placed before the verb or attached at the end of it.

Mi for *me* as in *lei mi chiama* (*she calls me*) or *chiamami* (*call me*)

Ti for *you* as in *I bambini ti vedono* (*the children see you*) or *io posso vederti* (*I can see you*)

La for *her/it* as in *io la conosco* (*I know her*) or *mangiala* (*eat it*) referring to *mela* (*apple*) for example

Lo for *him/it* as in *io lo conosco* (*I know him*) or *mangialo* (*eat it*) referring to *gelato* (*ice cream*)

Ci for *us* as in *tu ci vedi* (*you see us*) or *chiamaci* (*call us*)

Vi for *you* (many) as in *io vi vedo* or *loro vogliono invitarvi* (*they want to invite you* – many)

Li for *them* (masc. or both masc. and fem.) as in *li vedo domani* (*I see them tomorrow*) or *invitali* (*invite them*)

Le for *them* (fem.) as in *le vedo domani* (*I see them tomorrow*) or *invitale* (*invite them*)

Indirect object pronouns

When something or a person is indirectly affected by an action in English, you often (not always) use *to* with the pronoun: *I sent it to them yesterday, they awarded him a medal.* In Italian, you either use, as in English, a preposition *a* (*to*) followed by the appropriate direct pronoun or a set of indirect pronouns may stand in for indirect objects:

Mi or *a me* for *to me*

Ti or *a te* for *to you*

Gli or *a lui* for *to him*

Le or *a lei* for *to her*

Ci or *a noi* for *to us*

Vi or *a voi* for *to you* (many)

Li or *a loro* for *to them* (masc.)

Le or *a loro* for *to them* (fem.)

Le mando dei fiori for *I send her some flowers*

Posso mandarle dei fiori for *I can send her some flowers*

Double pronouns

You may need to use both a direct and indirect object pronoun, like in *he will bring it* (direct) *to me* (indirect). In Italian, the position of the double object pronoun will be as when they are by themselves: before the verb or attached to the infinitive verb. Most of the time, the direct precedes the indirect, like in English: *it* (direct) *to me* (indirect).

Most notably, when they are together, the indirect object pronoun changes to distinguish itself from the direct one:

Mi becomes *me* for *to me*

Ti becomes *te* for *to you*

Gli and *le* become *glie* for *to him* or *to her*

Ci becomes *ce* for *to us*

Vi becomes *ve* for *to you* (many)

Li and *le* become *glie* for *to them*

Instead of **Giovanni porta il libro a Mario** (*John brings the book to Mario*) you can say:

Giovanni glielo porta for *John brings it to him*

Instead of **lui legge la lettera a me** (*he reads the letter to me*), you can say:

Lui me la legge for *he reads it to me*

Instead of saying **voglio mandarti un regalo** (*I want to send you a gift*) you can say:

Voglio mandartelo for *I want to send it to you*

Possessive pronouns:

Possessives adjectives, like articles, must agree with the gender and number of the noun they modify. They can also replace a noun and become a possessive pronoun. In this case, they keep the article of the noun that they stand for:

Questa macchina è la mia for *this car is mine*

Se la tua macchina non funziona, puoi usare la mia for *if your car does not work, you can use mine*

Se il mio libro è noioso, puoi leggere il suo for *if my book is boring, you can read hers/his*

You can use a possessive pronoun to indicate part of a group: *one of mine* (*uno dei miei*), *one of my daughters is sick* (*una delle mie figlie è malata*), *three of my apple trees died* (*tre dei miei alberi di mele sono morti*).

Relative Pronouns:

Relative pronouns are used to connect clauses or phrases to nouns or pronouns. The pronoun can refer to a person, thing, or situation—like in English when you use *who, which, that, whom, where.*

The Italian relative pronouns are:

Che for *which, who* and *that* as a subject or direct object

Cui for *which, who and that* after a preposition in place for an indirect object

La ragazza che sta parlando è la figlia del direttore for *the girl who is speaking is the director's daughter*

La ragazza che stai guardando è la figlia del direttore for *the girl that you are watching is the director's daughter*

Questa è la canzone di cui ti parlavo for *this is the song that I was telling you about*

La pianta da cui è tratto lo zucchero for *the plant from which the sugar is extracted*

Quale for *who, whom, which, that* varies in gender and number and is preceded by an appropriate article:

Ho parlato con i suoi amici, i quali sostengono di non averlo visto

I spoke with his friends, who maintain they have not seen him

Demonstrative pronouns:

Demonstrative adjectives can be used as pronouns to refer to something specific in the context, often not to repeat the same word. The difference is that the adjective takes the place of the noun instead of accompanying it.

Questo, questa, questi, queste for *this* (masculine and feminine) and *these* (masculine and feminine)

Quello, quella, quelli, quelle for *that* (masculine and feminine) and *those* (masculine and feminine)

L'inverno passato è stato mite, questo è molto più freddo

The past winter was mild, this is much colder

Questo è un colabrodo

This is a colander

Questa è l'ultima volta che ti chiedo di venire

This is the last time I ask you to come

Questo è rotto

This is broken

Ci and *ne*

Ci and *ne* are two extremely common pronouns that have no single equivalent in English.

Ci is used to mean *it* or *about it* and usually comes before the verb, in an order, attached at the end of the infinitive:

Ripensandoci me ne sono pentito for *when I thought it over, I was sorry*

Non ci credo per niente for *I do not believe it at all*

Ci penserò for *I will think about it*

Non ci capisco niente for *I cannot understand it at all*

Non so che farci for *I do not know what to do about it*

Ci is used with the verb *entrare* (*to go* inside) in some common idiomatic phrases:

Cosa c'entra? for *what's going on with it?*

Io non c'entro for *this has nothing to do with me*

With *volere* (*to want*), meaning that something is necessary:

Ci vuole buona volontà for *goodwill is necessary*

Ci vogliono tre uova per fare la torta for *three eggs are necessary to make the cake*

With *mettere* (*to* put) becomes *metterci* (*to take*)

Ci si mette mezz'ora dal centro alla spiaggia for *it takes half an hour form the center to the beach*

With *vedere* (*to see*) becomes *vederci* (*to see each other*)

Ci vediamo tra mezz'ora for *let us meet in half an hour*

With **sentire** *(to hear)* becomes *sentirci* (*to hear from each other*)

Sentiamoci questa sera for *let us hear each other tonight*

Ne often replaces a noun and means *about it/about them, of it/of them, with it/with them*, and so on. When used with Italian adjectives or verbs which are followed by **di**, for example **contento di** (*happy about*), **stufo di** (*fed up with*), **aver paura di** (*to be afraid of*), **scrivere di** (*to write about*):

Ne sono molto contenta for *I am very happy about it*

Sono stufo di leggere solo giornali for *I am fed up about reading only newspapers*

Sono sicura di volere andare a Roma for *I am sure I want to go to Rome*

It can refer to amounts and quantities.

Ne vuoi? For *would you like some?*

Ne ho preso la metà for *I have taken half of it*

Ne can be used to refer to nouns that have already been mentioned.

Parliamone for *let's talk about it*

Verbs

Verbs describe events, like somebody performing an action (***Maria gioca con la palla***, *Maria plays with the ball*) or something happening (***piove***, *it rains*). Events happen at a particular time: in the present, past or future, and the form that a verb takes to express time is called tense. Italian verbs change their endings depending on the tense (i.e., when the event occurs): ***credo*** means *I believe*, ***credevo*** means *I believed* and ***crederò*** means *I will believe*. Italian verb endings also change according to who or what is doing the action (i.e., the subject of the verb) and it can be expressed by either a noun or pronoun: <u>Jack</u> *speaks Italian*; <u>She</u> *is playing tennis.*

In Italian, the citation form of a verb is the infinitive, which works as a noun as well: ***parlare*** can stand for *to speak* or *speaking* (***parlare è stancante*** for *speaking is tiring*). The last three letters of the infinitive (***-are, -ere, -ire***) determine the conjugation the verb belongs to and consequently the ending for each person in each tense. To conjugate a verb ending in –are, like ***parlare*** (*to speak*), you drop the ending ***-are*** and keep the stem ***parl-*** and add the inflections for each person.

While the conjugation of regular verbs consistently follows the same rules, irregular verbs do not follow the usual patterns. These irregular Italian verbs include very common and frequently used verbs such as ***andare*** (*to go*), ***essere*** (*to be*), and ***fare*** (*to do* or *to make*).

Auxiliary verbs: *essere* (*to be*) and *avere* (*to have*)

Like in English, auxiliary verbs are used in forming the tenses, moods, and voices of other verbs (like *be* and *have* in *I am going, you have gone, did you go?*).

As in English, Italian auxiliary verbs are *essere* (*to be*) and *avere* (*to have*); they have their own meaning (*io sono uno studente*/*I am a student* or *tu hai un cappello*/*you have a hat*) and they have an irregular conjugation. The simple tenses (present, imperfect...) are conjugated without an auxiliary, whereas the compound tenses (past and future) are formed with the help of an auxiliary: *io ho guardato* (*I have watched*), *io avrò guardato* (*I will have looked*), *io avevo guardato* (*I had looked*).

Ieri ho mangiato una pizza al formaggio for *yesterday I have eaten a pizza with cheese*

Sono arrivato oggi for *I arrived today*

Simple Present of *essere* (*to be*) and *avere* (*to have*):

Io sono for *I am*

Tu sei for *you are*

Lui/lei è for *she/he is*

Noi siamo for *we are*

Voi siete for *you (more than one) are*

Essi/loro sono for *they are*

Io ho* for *I have*

Tu hai* for *you have*

Lei/lui ha* for *she/he has*

Noi abbiamo for *we have*

Voi avete for *you have*

Loro/essi hanno* for *they have*

*Remember the *h* is always silent

Future of *essere* (*to be*) and *avere* (*to have*):

Io sarò for *I will be*

Tu sarai for *you will be*

Lei/lui sarà for *she/he will be*

Noi saremo for *we will be*

Voi sarete for *you* (many) *will be*

Essi saranno for *they will be*

Io avrò for *I will have*

Tu avrai for *you will have*

Lei/lui avrà for *she/he will have*

Noi avremo for *we will have*

Voi avrete for *you* (many) *will have*

Essi/loro avranno for *they will have*

The imperfect (expresses an ongoing action in the past) of *essere* (*to be*) and *avere* (*to have*):

Io ero for *I was*

Tu eri for *you were*

Lei/lui era for *she/he was*

Noi eravamo for *we were*

Voi eravate for *you* (many) *were*

Essi/loro erano for *they were*

Io avevo for *I had*

Tu avevi for *you had*

Lei/lui aveva for *she/he had*

Noi avevamo for *we had*

Voi avevate for *you* (many) *had*

Essi/loro avevano for *they had*

The present perfect of *essere* (*to be*) and *avere* (*to have*):

The present perfect indicates actions completed in the recent past and often followed by expressions like (*ieri*/*yesterday*, *domenica*/*Sunday*, *un'ora fa*/*an hour ago*, *un anno fa*/*a year ago*). This is a compound tense formed by the present of either *essere* or *avere* followed by the past participle of the verb.

The participle agrees with the subject number and gender: *stato*, *stata*, *stati*, *state* (*been*) for singular masculine and feminine and plural masculine and feminine of *essere* and *avuto*, *avuta*, *avuti*, *avute* (*had*) for singular masculine and feminine and plural masculine and feminine of *avere*.

Io sono stato for *I was*

Tu sei stato for *you were*

Lei è stata/lui è stato for *she/he was*

Noi siamo stati for *we were*

Voi siete stati for *you* (many) *were*

Essi/loro sono stati for *they were*

Io ho avuto for I *had*

Tu hai avuto for *you had*

Lui/lei ha avuto for *she/he had*

Noi abbiamo avuto for *we had*

Voi avete avuto for *you* (many) *had*

Essi/loro hanno avuto for *they had*

As for other verbs, the past participle of verbs of motions (*andare*/*to go*, *partire*/*to leave*) and states (*nascere*/*to be born*) usually goes with the present of *essere*, whereas the past participle of transitive verbs (*mangiare*/*to eat*, *scrivere*/*to write*, *vendere*/*to sell*) follow the present of *avere*.

Regular verbs

Regular verbs in Italian are predictably conjugated in the same way: their ending changes consistently depending on their conjugation (the class they belong to), the person who is performing the action, and the tense (the time when the action occurs).

To conjugate a regular verb, you drop the ending *-are*, *-ere* or *-ire* for *parl-are* (*to speak*), *chied-ere* (*to ask*), *sent-ire* (*to hear*) or *cap-*ire (*to* understand), keep the stem *parl-*, and add the inflections for each person in a particular tense. Every regular verb ending in *-are* will take the same ending for the same person in the same tense and so will those ending in *-ere* and *-ire*.

Simple Present of *-are*: *-o, -i, -a, -iamo, -ate, -ano*

Io parlo for *I speak*

Tu parli for *you speak*

Lei/lui parla for *she/he speaks*

Noi parliamo for *we speak*

Voi parlate for *you* (many) *speak*

Essi/loro parlano for *they speak*

Simple Present of *-ere*: *-o, -i, -e, -iamo, -ete, -edono*

Io chiedo for *I ask*

Tu chiedi for *you ask*

Lei/lui chiede for *she/he asks*

Noi chiediamo for *we ask*

Voi chiedete for *you* (many) *ask*

Essi/loro chiedono for *they ask*

Simple Present of *-ire*: *-o, -i, -e, -iamo, -ite, -ono*

Io sento for *I hear*

Tu senti for *you hear*

Lei/lui sente for *she/he hear*

Noi sentiamo for *we hear*

Voi sentite for *you (many) hear*

Essi/loro sentono for *they hear*

Simple Present of *-ire*: *-isco, -isci, -isce, -iamo, -ite, -iscono*

Io finisco for *I finish*

Tu finisci for *you finish*

Lei/lui finisce for *she/he finish*

Noi finiamo for *we finish*

Voi finite for *you* (many) *finish*

Essi/loro finiscono for *they finish*

The imperfect of regular verbs *-are, -ere, -ire*:

Io parlavo for *I was talking*

Tu parlavi for *you were talking*

Lui/lei parlava for *she/he was talking*

Noi parlavamo for *we were talking*

Voi parlavate for *you* (many) *were talking*

Essi/loro parlavano for *they were talking*

Io chiedevo for *I was asking*

Tu chiedevi for *you were asking*

Lei/lui chiedeva for *she/he was asking*

Noi chiedevamo for *we were asking*

Voi chiedevate for *you* (many) *were asking*

Essi/loro chiedevano for *they were asking*

Io capivo for *I was understanding*

Tu capivi for *you were understanding*

Lei/lui capiva for *she/he was understanding*

Noi capivamo for *we were understanding*

Voi capivate for *you* (many) *were understanding*

Loro/essi capivano for *they were understanding*

The future of regular verbs *-are, -ere, -ire*:

Io parlerò for *I will speak*

Tu parlerai for *you will speak*

Lei/lui parlerà for *she/he will speak*

Noi parleremo for *we will speak*

Voi parlerete for *you* (many) *will speak*

Essi/loro parleranno for *they will speak*

Io chiederò for *I will ask*

Tu chiederai for *you will ask*

Lei/lui chiederà for *she/he will ask*

Noi chiederemo for *we will ask*

Voi chiederete for *you* (many) *will ask*

Essi/loro chiederanno for *they will ask*

Io capirò for *I will understand*

Tu capirai for *you will understand*

Lei/lui capirà for *she/he will understand*

Noi capiremo for *we will understand*

Voi capirete for *you* (many) *will understand*

Essi/loro capiranno for *they will understand*

Frequently used verbs in -*are*: *abitare* (*to leave*), *arrivare* (*to arrive*), *ascoltare* (*to listen*), *aspettare* (*to wait*), *camminare* (*to walk*), *cenare* (*to have dinner*), *comprare* (*to buy*), *domandare* (*to ask*), *entrare* (*to enter*), *guardare* (*to look*), *lavorare* (*to work*), *nuotare* (*to swim*), *ordinare* (*to order*), *pranzare* (*to have lunch*), *riposare* (*to rest*), *prenotare* (*to reserve*).

Frequently used verbs for -*ere*: *chiudere* (*to close*), *credere* (*to believe*), *leggere* (*to read*), *perdere* (*lo lose*), *piangere* (*to cry*), *ripetere* (*to repeat*), *rispondere* (*to answer*), *rompere* (*to break*), *scrivere* (*to write*), *vendere* (*to sell*), *vivere* (*to live*).

Frequently used verbs in the first type of -*ire*: *aprire* (*to open*), *coprire* (*to cover*), *dormire* (*to sleep*), *offrire* (*to offer*), *partire* (*to leave*), *scoprire* (*to discover*), *seguire* (*to follow*), *servire* (*to serve*), *vestire* (*to dress*).

The past participle of regular verbs and their Present perfect

To produce the present perfect you need to know the past participle of the verb. To form the past participle of regular verbs in -*are*, -*ere* and -*ire,* you add -*ato*, -*uto* and -*ito* to the stem respectively:

Parlare becomes *parlato* for *to speak* becomes *spoken*

Vendere becomes *venduto* for *to sell* becomes *sold*

Partire becomes *partito* for *to leave* becomes *left*

The present perfect of regular verbs -*are*, -*ere*, -*ire*:

Io ho parlato for *I spoke*

Tu hai parlato for you spoke

Lui/lei ha parlato for *she/he spoke*

Noi abbiamo parlato for *we spoke*

Voi avete parlato for *you (many) spoke*

Essi/loro hanno parlato for *they spoke*

Io ho chiesto for *I asked*

Tu hai chiesto for *you asked*

Lei/lui ha chiesto for *she/he asked*

Noi abbiamo chiesto for *we asked*

Voi avete chiesto for *you* (many) *asked*

Essi/loro hanno chiesto for *they asked*

Io ho finito for *I finished*

Tu hai finito for *you finished*

Lei/lui ha finito for *she/he finished*

Noi abbiamo finito for *we finished*

Voi avete finito for *you (many) finished*

Essi/loro hanno finito for *they finished*

Gerund and the present progressive

The gerund is used to express an action simultaneous to another: *camminando*, *while walking*. It can therefore also be used to express an ongoing action in the present, past, and future. For the present progressive, the gerund of a verb follows the simple present of the verb stare:

Io sto camminando for *I am walking*

Tu stai camminando for *you are walking*

Lei/lui sta camminando for *she/he is walking*

Noi stiamo camminando for *we are walking*

Voi state camminando for *you* (many) *are walking*

Essi/loro stanno camminando for *they are walking*

Verbs ending in *-are* will add to the stem *-ando*, those ending in *-ere* and *-ire* will add *-endo* (*correre* and *correndo* for *to run* and *while running*, *dormire* and *dormendo* for *to sleep* and *while sleeping*).

Irregular verbs

Irregular verbs are verbs that do not follow fully or at all the rules of the conjugation of the class they belong to.

Most frequent irregular verbs ending in -are are:

Simple Present of *andare* (*to go*), *dare* (*to give*), *fare* (*to do/to make*), *stare* (*to stay*):

Io vado for *I go*

Tu vai for *you go*

Lei/lui va for *she/he goes*

Noi andiamo for *we go*

Voi andate for *you* (many) *go*

Essi/loro vanno for *they go*

Io do for *I give*

Tu dai for *you give*

Lei/lui dà for *she/he gives*

Noi diamo for *we give*

Voi date for *you* (many) *give*

Essi/loro danno for *they give*

Io faccio for *I do*

Tu fai for *you do*

Lui/lei fa for *she/he does*

Noi facciamo for *we do*

Voi fate for *you* (many) *do*

Essi/loro fanno for *they do*

Io sto for *I stay*

Tu stai for *you stay*

Lei/lui sta for *she/he stays*

Noi stiamo for *we stay*

Voi state for *you* (many) *stay*

Essi/loro stanno for *they stay*

Simple Present of **bere** (*to drink*), **sapere** (*to know*), **spegnere** (*to turn off*), and **tenere** (*to keep*):

Io bevo for *I drink*

Tu bevi for *you drink*

Lei/lui beve for *she/he drink*

Noi beviamo for *we drink*

Voi bevete for *you* (many) *drink*

Essi/loro bevono for *they drink*

Io so for *I know*

Tu sai for *you know*

Lei/lui sa for *she/he knows*

Noi sappiamo for *we know*

Voi sapete for *you* (many) *know*

Essi/loro sanno for *they know*

Io spengo for *I turn off*

Tu spegni for *you turn off*

Lei/lui spegne for *she/he turns off*

Noi spegniamo for *we turn off*

Voi spegnete for *you (many) turn off*

Essi/loro spengono for *they turn off*

Io tengo for *I keep*

Tu tieni for *you keep*

Lei/lui tiene for *she/he keeps*

Noi teniamo for *we keep*

Voi tenete for *you (many) keep*

Essi/loro tengono for *they keep*

Simple Present of **dire** (*to say*), **morire** (*to die*), **salire** (*to go up*), and **uscire** (*to go out*), **venire** (*to come*):

Io dico for *I say*

Tu dici for *you say*

Lei/lui dice for *she/he says*

Noi diciamo for *we say*

Voi dite for *you* (many) *say*

Essi/loro dicono for *they say*

Io muoio for *I die*

Tu muori for *you die*

Lei/lui muore for *she/he dies*

Noi moriamo for *we die*

Voi morite for *you* (many) *die*

Essi/loro muoiono for *they die*

Io salgo for *I go up*

Tu sali for *you go up*

Lei/lui sale for *she/he goes up*

Noi saliamo for *we go up*

Voi salite for *you* (many) *go up*

Essi/loro salgono for *they go up*

Io esco for *I go out*

Tu esci for *you go out*

Lei/lui esce for *she/he goes out*

Noi usciamo for *we go out*

Voi uscite for *you* (many) *go out*

Essi/loro escono for *they go out*

Io vengo for *I come*

Tu vieni for *you come*

Lei/lui viene for *she/he comes*

Noi veniamo for *we come*

Voi venite for *you* (many) *come*

Essi/loro vengono for *they come*

Modal verbs

There are three modal verbs in Italian: **volere** (*to want*), **potere** (*to want/to be able to*) e **dovere** (*to must, to have to*). They have an irregular conjugation in the Simple Present and a very particular construction in the Present Perfect.

Simple Present of **volere** (*to want*), **potere** (*can/to be able to*) e **dovere** (*to must, to have to*):

Io voglio for *I want*

Tu vuoi for *you want*

Lei/lui vuole for *she/he wants*

Noi vogliamo for *we want*

Voi volete for *you* (many) *want*

Loro/essi vogliono for *they want*

Io posso for *I can/am able to*

Tu puoi for *you can/are able to*

Lei/lui può for *she/he can/is able to*

Noi possiamo for *we can/are able to*

Voi potete for *you* (many) *can/are able to*

Loro/essi possono for *they can/are able to*

Io devo for *I must/have to*

Tu devi for *you must/have to*

Lei/lei deve for *she/he must/have to*

Noi dobbiamo for *we must/have to*

Voi dovete for *you* (many) *must/have to*

Loro/essi devono for *they must/have to*

These three verbs may be used on their own or used with another verb indicating which action somebody wants, can or has to perform: *io voglio/posso/devo suonare il piano* (*I want to/am able to/have to play the piano*). In this case, they require a special construction in the Present Perfect. The choice of the auxiliary verb (i.e., *essere* or *avere*) depends on the verb that follows the modal verb:

Ho voluto finire il lavoro for *I wanted to finish the work*

Sono voluto andare al cinema for *I wanted to go to the cinema*

Ho dovuto rimandare l'appuntamento for *I had to postpone the appointment*

È dovuto andare dal dottore for *he had to go to the doctor*

Ho potuto mangiare il gelato for *I could eat the ice cream*

È potuta partire di domenica for *she could leave on Sunday*

Reflexive verbs

The subject and the object of reflexive verbs are the same person! It sounds complicated, but this is what happens when *you wash yourself*: Who performs and who receives the action are the same person.

The infinitive of reflexive Italian verbs ends in *-arsi, -ersi*, and *-irsi*:

Svegliarsi for *to wake oneself up*

Nutrirsi for *to feed oneself*

Abituarsi for *to get used (yourself) to something*

Chiamarsi for *to be named (literally: to call oneself)*

Chiedersi for *to ask oneself*

Divertirsi for *to have fun*

Prepararsi for *to get ready*

Dimenticarsi for *to forget*

Domandarsi for *to wonder*

Presentarsi for *to introduce oneself*

Addormentarsi for *to fall asleep*

Alzarsi for *to get up*

Ammalarsi for *to get sick*

Riposarsi for *to rest*

Sedersi for *to sit*

Approffitarsi (di) for *to take advantage of*

Bruciarsi con for *to get burned with*

Fidarsi di for *to trust*

Incontrarsi con for *to meet with*

Lamentarsi di for *to complain about*

These verbs are conjugated like the regular (-are, -ere and -ire) and are preceded by the reflexive pronoun that matches the subject:

Io mi alzo for *I get up*

Tu ti alzi for *you get up*

Lei/lui si alza for *she/he gets up*

Noi ci alziamo for *we get up*

Voi vi alzate for *you* (many) *get up*

Essi/loro si alzano for *they get up*

The reflexive pronoun is usually in front of the verb, but it can also attach to the end of the infinitive after modal verbs:

Lei vuole seder<u>si</u> sull'erba for *she wants to sit on the grass*

Noi dobbiamo prepara<u>rci</u> per l'esame for *we have to prepare for the test*

Reflexive verbs more often concern people:

Vestirsi for *to get dressed*

Svestirsi for *to get undressed*

Spazzolarsi for *to brush (teeth or hair)*

Farsi il bagno/la doccia/la barba for *to take a bath/a shower/ to shave*

Truccarsi for *to put on makeup*

Arrabbiarsi for *to become angry*

Calmarsi for *to calm down*

Irritarsi for *to get irritated*

Preoccuparsi for *to worry*

Rallegrarsi for *to rejoice*

Spaventarsi for *to get frightened*

Chiamarsi (*to be named*)

When introducing yourself or somebody else, you use the verb *chiamarsi* (literally *to call oneself*).

Simple Present:

Io mi chiamo means *my name is* (literally: *I call myself*)

Tu ti chiami for *your name is* (literally: *you call yourself*)

Lei/lui si chiama for *her/his name is* (literally: *she/he calls herself/himself*)

Noi ci chiamiamo for *our names are* (literally: *we call ourselves*)

Voi vi chiamate for *your names are* (literally: *you call yourselves*)

Loro/essi si chiamano for *their names are* (literally: *you call yourselves*)

Mi chiamo Lara for *my name is Lara*

Lei come si chiama? for *what is your name?* (formal)

Tu come ti chiami? for *what is your name?* (informal)

Noi ci chiamiamo Paolo e Mara, voi come vi chiamate? For *our names are Paolo and Mara, what are your names?*

Reciprocal reflexive verbs

To express reciprocity, you can use the plural form of reflexive verbs:

Vedersi (*to see each other*):

I bambini si vedono ogni giorno for *the children see each other every day*

Amarsi (*to love each other*):

Francesca e Giovanni si amano molto for *Francesca e Giovanni love each other very much*

Capirsi (*to understand each other*)

I fratelli si capiscono bene for *the brothers understand each other well*

Conoscersi for *to know each other*

Aiutarsi for *to help each other*

Parlarsi for *to talk to each other*

Scriversi for *to write to each other*

Verbs with indirect object

Most verbs take both a direct and an indirect object. A direct object is the receiver of an action within a sentence; in *I throw the ball, the ball* receives the action of being thrown. In *I send you a letter, the letter* is the receiver of the action of being sent and *you* are the person for whom the action is performed: the indirect object. The indirect object identifies to or for whom or what the action of the verb is performed.

As in English, few Italian verbs take only indirect objects. For example, both in English and in Italian, *to happen* (**accadere**) only has an indirect object: *many beautiful things are happening to me* (*mi stanno accadendo molte cose belle*); or *what is happening to you?* (**Cosa ti accade?**).

Verbs with an indirect object are common and may be very useful to know how to use:

Piacere for *to like*

Accadere for *to happen*

Bastare for *to be enough/sufficient*

Dispiacere for *to regret*

Dolere for *to suffer*

Importare for *to matter/to be important*

Interessare for *to interest*

Sembrare for *to seem*

Servire for *to need*

Some might have a different construction from their English translation, and this might become confusing, like in the case of *piacere* (*to like*), whose English counterpart takes a direct object. The easiest way of approaching the use of *piacere* is to keep translating it with *to be pleasing* [to somebody].

Simple Present of *piacere* (*to like*):

Io piaccio for *I am pleasing to*

Tu piaci for *you are pleasing to*

Lei/lui piace for *she/he is pleasing to*

Noi piaciamo for *we are pleasing to*

Voi piacete for *you* (many) *are pleasing to*

Essi/loro piacciono for *they are pleasing to*

You may just say the *you are pleasing* (*tu piaci*), meaning they you are quite attractive or entertaining; more often, though, you might need to mention who is receiving the action: *io piaccio al postino* (*I am pleasing to the mailman/the mailman likes me*). As a result, these verbs are very often used with indirect pronouns: *mi* or *a me* (*to me*), *ti* or *a te*, *le* or *a lei* (*to her*), *gli* or *a lui* (*to him*), *ci* or *a noi* (*to us*), *vi* or *a voi* (*to you* – many), *le* or *a loro* (*to them* – feminine) and *li* or *a loro* (*to them* – masculine).

Io ti piaccio for *I am pleasing to you* (i.e., *you like me*)

Tu mi piaci for *you are pleasing to me* (i.e., *I like you*)

Le piace la pizza for *the pizza is pleasing to her* (i.e., *she likes the pizza*)

Vi piacciono i libri for *the books are pleasing to you* (i.e., *you – many – like the books*)

Ci piace passeggiare for *walking is pleasing to us* (i.e., *we like walking*)

The other verbs behave similarly:

Accadere for *to happen* as in *questo mi accade sempre* for *this always happens to me*

Bastare for *to be enough/sufficient* as in *il caffè mi basta* for *the coffee is enough*

Dispiacere for *to regret* as in *le dispiace partire* for *she regrets to leave*

Dolere for *to suffer* as in *ti duole la testa* for your head hurts (to you)

Importare for *to matter/to be important* as in *questo non ci importa* for *this does not matter to us*

Interessare for *to interest* as in *il museo vi interessa molto* for *the museum is very interesting to you*

Sembrare for *to seem* as in *mi sembra un bravo ragazzo* for *he seems like a good boy to me*

Servire for *to need* as in *le serve il tuo aiuto* for *she needs your help*

Adverbs and prepositions

Adverbs modify or specify a particular aspect of an event, and they refer to a verb: *I run fast*. They can also determine the meaning of an adjective (***molto** **buono*** for *very good*) or the meaning of another adverb (***troppo velocemente*** for *too fast*). There are different kind of adverbs depending on which aspect of the meaning they specify and different types more commonly either precede or follow the verb.

Adverbs of time usually precede the verb: *adesso* (*now*), *allora* (*then*), *appena* (*as soon as possible*), *domani* (*tomorrow*), *oggi* (*today*), *ieri* (*yesterday*), *dopo* (*later*), *fino a* (*until*), *finora* (*until now*), *già* (*already*), *mai* (*never*), *ogni tanto* (*every once in a while*), *ora* (*now*), *poi* (*then*), *presto* (*soon*), *raramente* (*rarely*), *sempre* (*always*), *tardi* (*late*).

Adesso vado a casa for *now I go home*

Adverbs of quantity usually follow the verb: *troppo* (*too*), *poco* (*some/a little*), *abbastanza* (*enough*), *assai* (*very much*), *molto* (*much*), *tanto* (*so much/a lot*).

I bambini leggono troppo poco for *the children read too little*

Adverbs of location: *dappertutto* (*everywhere*), *davanti* (*in front*), *dietro* (*behind*), *fuori* (*outside*), *giù* (*down*), *indietro* (*behind/back*), *lì/là* (*there*), *lontano* (*far*), *ovunque* (*everywhere*), *qui/qua* (*here*), *sotto* (*under*), *su* (*up*), *vicino* (*near*).

Ti ho cercato dappertutto for *I looked for you everywhere*

Adverbs of manner: *bene* (*well*), *male* (*badly*), *forte* (*loudly/heavily*), *piano* (*slowly/quietly*), *tristemente* (*sadly*).

You can form many adverbs adding *-mente* to the stem of an adjective: *lenta* (*slow*) becomes *lentamente* (*slowly*). In the same way, in English, you add the ending *-ly* to an adjective: *slow* and *slowly*.

Fortunato (*lucky*) becomes *fortunatamente* (*luckily*)

Certo (*certain*) becomes *certamente* (*certainly*)

Onesto (*honest*) becomes *onestamente* (*honestly*)

Provvisorio (*temporary*) becomes *provvisoriamente* (*temporarily*)

Silenzioso (*quiet*) becomes *silenziosamente* (*quietly*)

Ultimo (*last*) becomes *ultimamente* (*lastly*)

Altro (*other*) becomes *altrimenti* (*otherwise*)

Leggero (*light*) becomes *leggermente* (*lightly*)

Dolce (*sweet*) becomes *dolcemente* (*sweetly*)

Felice (*happy*) becomes *felicemente* (*happily*)

Frequente (*frequent*) becomes *frequentemente* (*frequently*)

Facile (*easy*) becomes *facilmente* (*easily*)

Gentile (*kind*) becomes **gentilmente** (*kindly*)

Like adjectives, adverbs have comparatives and superlatives. Comparatives can be constructed by adding **più** (*more*), **meno** (*less*), or **tanto... quanto** (*as much as*) before the adverb:

Velocemente (*quickly*) becomes **più velocemente** and **meno** *velocemente* and **tanto velocemente quanto**

Superlatives are made by adding -issim before -mente (**velocissimamente**), or **il più** before the adverb (**il più velocemente**) for *the fastest.*

In Italian, you can use adverbial expressions with the prepositions *a, di, da, in*:

In alto for *up high*

In basso for *down*

In breve for *in short*

A destra for *to the right*

In generale for *generally*

Da lontano for *from a distance*

A lungo for *at length*

In mezzo for *in the middle*

Di nuovo for *again*

In orario for *on time*

Di recente for *recently*

In ritardo for *late*

A sinistra for *to the left*

Di solito for *usually*

Da vicino for *close up*

All'improvviso for *all of a sudden*

Prepositions

Prepositions are words that precede a noun, a pronoun, an adverb, or an infinitive verb, and specify its function, expressing locations, possession, cause, manner, or purpose: *il biscotto nel piatto* (*the cookie in the plate*), *il menù del ristorante* (*the menu of the restaurant*), *studia per imparare* (*he studies to learn*), *la torta è per la nonna* (*the cake is for the grandmother*). There are three kinds of prepositions: proper, improper, articulated.

Proper prepositions: *di* (*of*), *a* (*at/to*), *da* (*from/at*), *in* (*in*), *con* (*with*), *su* (*on*), *per* (*for/in order to*), *tra* or *fra* (*among/in between*).

La casa di Pietro for *Peter's house*

Sono a casa for *I am at home*

Vado a Roma for *I go to Rome*

Arrivo da Londra for *I arrive from London*

Improper prepositions may be adjectives or adverbs used as prepositions:

Senza (*without*), **contro** (*against*), **durante** (*during*), **eccetto** (*except*), **fino** a (*until*), **secondo** (*according to*), **tranne** (*except*)...

Durante il concerto ha iniziato a piovere for *during the concert it started raining*

Abbiamo visitato tutti i musei eccetto uno for *we visited every museum except one*

Articulated prepositions:

The prepositions *di, a, da, in, su* e *con* become articulated: they blend with the article that follows them when they modify a noun that requires an article (*il, lo, la, i, gli, le*). *Per, tra*, and *fra* have just the simple form.

Di becomes *del, dello, della, dei, degli, delle*

A becomes *al, allo, alla, ai, agli, alle*

Da becomes *dal, dallo, dalla, dai, dagli, dalle*

In becomes *nel, nello, nella, nei, negli, nelle*

Su becomes *sul, sullo, sulla, sui, sugli, sulle*

Con only blends with *il* and becomes *col*.

Interrogatives and negatives

Asking questions in Italian is really easy: there are no differences the way the words are sequenced, the change that occurs when placing a question mark at the end of the statement is one of intonation, and the voice rises at the end of the sentence.

The conditional is polite!

To ask for something politely, when ordering at the restaurant, on the plane, buying tickets, asking for directions, in Italian, you use the conditional of *volere* (*to want*) which corresponds to using *would*, but often translates as *would like*:

Present Indicative:

Io voglio for *I want*

Tu vuoi for *you want*

Lei/lui vuole for *she/he wants*

Noi vogliamo for *we want*

Voi volete for *you* (many) *want*

Essi/loro vogliono for *they want*

Present Conditional:

Io vorrei for *I would*

Tu vorresti for *you would*

Lei/lui vorrebbe for *she/he would*

Noi vorremmo for *we would*

Voi vorreste for *you would*

Essi/loro vorrebbero for *they would*

Indirect questions

Indirect questions are questions embedded in other sentences and can provide another polite way of asking a question or simply a way of reporting a question:

Vorrei sapere se la stazione è da questa parte

I would like to know whether the station is this way

Mi domando se questa è la strada giusta

I wonder whether this is the right way

Mi chiedo se il tempo resterà bello

I wonder whether the weather will still be beautiful

Potresti dirmi dov'è la stazione?

Could you tell me where is the station?

Posso chiederle se domani il treno partirà in orario?

May I ask you whether tomorrow the train will leave on time?

Le ho chiesto se il negozio era aperto

I asked her whether the store was open

Is there / are there?

Often in English, *is there?* and *are there?* are used to ask for something that you are looking for, such as a restaurant, a restroom, a taxi. The expressions *c'è* and *ci sono* correspond to the English *there is* and *there are* respectively. These words are used in the same order to both state there is something there and to ask: is there something? A rising tone for the question makes the difference:

C'è un ristorante vicino all'albergo for *there is a restaurant close to the hotel*

Ci sono dei negozi vicino ala stazione for *there are some stores nearby the station*

C'è un ristorante vicino al teatro? for *is there a restaurant close to the theater?*

Ci sono dei negozi vicino al museo? for *are there some stores nearby the museum?*

C'è, ci sono, ecco

C'è (*there is*) and *ci sono* (*there are*) are extremely frequent expressions in Italian. They are used to indicate the presence of people, animals, or things:

C'è (*there is*) is used to refer to the presence of a single element:

Guarda, c'è un gatto sul tetto! for *look, there is a cat on the roof!*

In frigorifero c'è uno yogurt for *in the fridge there is a yogurt*

Oggi c'è il sole for *today it is sunny* (literally: today there is the sun)

ci sono (*there are*) is used to refer to many individuals or things

Ci sono due gatti sul tetto for *there are two cats on the roof*

In frigorifero ci sono ancora molti yogurt for *there are still many yogurts in the fridge*

C'è (*there is*) and *ci sono* (*there are*) are also used in negative and interrogative sentences:

Ci sono ancora dei biscotti al cioccolato? for *are there still some chocolate cookies?*

Non c'è più pane for *there isn't any bread*

The word *ecco* matches the English *here is* and *here are* (also *there is* and *there are*) and might be a likely answer to an *is there/are there* question:

Ci sono ancora due biglietti per il film? for *are there still two tickets for the movie?*

Ecco i biglietti for *here are the tickets*

C'è ancora un tavolo per quattro? for *is there still a table for four?*

Ecco il vostro tavolo for *here is your table*

Ecco il ristorante! for *here is the restaurant!*

Ecco il giornale! for *here is the newspaper!*

Ecco i calzini! for *here are the socks!*

Eccomi for *here I am*

Eccoti for *here you are*

Eccola for *here she is*

Eccolo for *here he is*

Eccoci for *here we are*

Eccovi for *here you (many) are*

Eccoli for *here they are (masculine)*

Eccole for here they are (feminine)

Interrogative Adverbs

Interrogative adverbs are invariable and do not agree with anything; the subject of the verb is usually placed at the end of the question:

come? for *how?*

com' in front of a vowel, i.e., *è* (*is*), *era* (*was*), *erano* (were)

come siete venuti in Italia, in aereo o in macchina? for *how did you come to Italy, by plane or by car?*

come mai for *how come?* or *why?*

come mai non potete restare un altro giorno con noi? for *how come you cannot stay another day with us?*

dove? for *where?*

dov' in front of a vowel like *è* (*is*), *era* (*was*), *erano* (were)

dove abitano i tuoi genitori? for *where do your parents live?*

dov'è andata in vacanza la professoressa? for *where did the professor go on vacation?*

perché? for *why?*

perché non venite a cena da noi un giorno? For *why don't you come over for dinner one day?*

quando? for *when?*

quando abbiamo l'esame finale in questa classe? for *when do we have the final test for this class?*

quanto? for *how much?*

quanto dura la classe di italiano? for *how long does the Italian class last?*

Interrogative Adjectives

Interrogative adjectives agree with the noun to which they refer, except for *che* (*which*) that is invariable

Che? for *what? what kind of?*

Che tipo di film preferiscono i tuoi genitori? for *what kind of movie do your parents prefer?*

Quale/quali? for *which? what?*

Qual in front of a vowel like *è* (*is*), *era* (*was*), *erano* (were)

Quali libri hai già letto? for *which books have you already read?*

Qual era il nome di tua madre prima di sposarsi? for *Which was your mother's name before getting married?*

Quanto, quanta, quanti, quante? for *how much? how many?*

Quanti libri hai letto durante le vacanze? for *how many books have you read during your vacation?*

Quanta pazienza hai con i bambini? for *how much patience do you have with children?*

Interrogative pronouns

Chi? for *who? whom?* always refers to people and is invariable

Chi è la tua attrice preferita? for *who is your favorite actress?*

Con chi siete usciti ieri sera? for *with whom did you go out last night?*

Di chi? for *whose?*

Di chi sono questi occhiali? for *whose are these glasses?*

Che, che cosa, cosa? for *what?* all mean the same thing and refer to things and are invariable

Cos' in front of a vowel, like *è* (*is*), *era* (*was*), *erano* (were)

Che farai durante le vacanze? for *what will you do during your holidays?*

Che cosa ti piace fare durante il tempo libero? for *what do you like to do in your spare time?*

Cosa piace ai genitori? for *what do parents like?*

Cos'è quel rumore? for *what is that noise?*

Quale, quali? for *which one, which ones?* refers to people, things, ideas

Qual in front of a vowel like *è* (*is*), *era* (*was*), *erano* (were)

Pallacanestro o calcio: quale preferisci? for *basketball or soccer, which do you prefer?*

quanto, quanta, quanti, quante? for *how much? how many?* refers to people or things

Quanto costa? for *how much does it cost?*

Ho visto molti film in Italia, tu quanti ne hai visti? for *I saw many movies in Italy, how many did you see?*

Negative sentences

In Italian, any sentence can be made negative by placing **non** (*not*) before the verb.

Questa città è grande (*this city is big*) becomes *questa città non è grande* (*this city is not big*).

With reflexive verbs, **non** precedes the reflexive pronouns as well:

Lui si pettina tutti i giorni (*he combs his hair every day*) becomes *non si pettina tutti i giorni* (*he does not comb his hair every day*).

With verbs with indirect objects, **non** (*not*) precedes the verbs but not the object unless the object is a pronoun:

A Maria non piace studiare for *Maria does not like studying*

Non le piace studiare for *she does not like studying*

Other words that make a negative sentence are: *nessuno* (*no one*), *niente* (*nothing*), *per niente* (*at all*), *mai* (*never*), *affatto* (*at all*), *neanche*, *nemmeno* and *neppure* (*not even*).

Nessuno sta correndo for *nobody is running*

Niente è del colore giusto for *nothing is of the right color*

Double negative in Italian

Unlike English, Italian often uses a double negative with **non** preceding the verb and another word expressing negation (*mai, nessuno, niente...*) following the verb:

Affatto for *at all:*

Il gelato non mi piace affatto for *I don't like ice cream at all*

Non ci penso affatto ad andare a teatro for *I am not thinking of going to the theater at all*

Mai for *never:*

Non studiamo mai il giovedì sera for *we never study on Thursday night*

Io non mangio mai la trippa for *I never eat the tripe*

Non... più for *no longer:*

Lui non lavora più ogni giorno for *he no longer works every day*

Non... ancora for *not yet:*

Non hai ancora fatto i compiti? for *haven't you done your homework yet?*

Neanche, nemmeno, neppure for *not even:*

Io non dico neanche una parola for *I don't even say a word*

Non studi nemmeno un'ora for *you don't even study for an hour*

Non fai neppure un pisolino for *you don't even take a nap*

Nessuno for *no one, nobody:*

Non abbiamo nessun amico in Italia for *we have no friends in Italy*

Niente for *nothing:*

Non ho niente nel frigorifero for *I have nothing in the fridge*

Per niente for *not at all:*

Non mi piace per niente for *I do not like it at all*

Non... né... né for *neither... nor:*

Lei non legge né libri né riviste for *she reads neither books nor magazines*

Chapter 10 - Essential Vocabulary

Italian – English

A for *at or to*

A volte for *sometimes*

Abbastanza for *enough*

Abitare for *to live*

Abituarsi for *to get used to something*

Accadere for *to happen*

Accanto for *next to*

Aceto (l'aceto, gli aceti) for *vinegar*

Acquario (l'acquario, gli acquari) for *aquarium*

Acquisto (l'acquisto, gli acquisti) for *purchase*

Addetto (l'addetto, gli addetti) for *clerk*

Addormentarsi for *to fall asleep*

Adesso for *now*

Aeroplano (l'aeroplano, gli aeroplani) *for airplane*

Aeroporto (l'aeroporto, gli aeroporti) *for airport*

Agenzia (l'agenzia, le agenzie) for *agency*

Agitato (agitato, agitati, agitata, agitate) for *rough*

Agosto for *August*

Agriturismo (l'agriturismo, gli agriturismi) *for farm holiday*

Aiutarsi *for to help each other*

Albergatore (l'albergatore, gli albergatori) for *hotel owner*

Albergo (l'albergo, gli alberghi) for *hotel*

Albicocca (l'albicocca, le albicocche) for *apricot*

Aliscafo (l'aliscafo, gli aliscafi) for *hydrofoil*

Allegro (allegro, allegri, allegra, allegre) for *happy*

Allora for *then*

Altrimenti *for otherwise*

Altro (altro, altri, altra, altre) for *other, another*

Alzarsi *for to get up*

Amarsi *for to love each other*

Amico (l'amico, gli amici, l'amica, le amiche) for *friend*

Ammalarsi *for to get sick*

Ammorbidente (l'ammorbidente, gli ammorbidenti) for *softener*

Analgesico (l'analgesico, gli analgesici) for *painkiller*

Analisi (l'analisi, le analisi) for *analysis*

Ananas (l'ananas, gli ananas) for *pineapple*

Andare bene for *to fit*

Andare for *to go*

Anello (l'anello, gli anelli) for *ring*

Anguria (l'anguria, le angurie) for *watermelon*

Animale (l'animale, gli animali) for *animal*

Anno (l'anno, gli anni) for *year*

Annullare for *to cancel*

Ano (l'ano, gli ani) for *anus*

Antipasto (l'antipasto, gli antipasti) for *appetizer*

Aperitivo (l'aperitivo, gli aperitivi) for *aperitif*

Appena for *as soon as possible*

Approfittarsi (di) for *to take advantage of*

Aprile for *April*

Aprire for *to open*

Aragosta (l'aragosta, le aragoste) for *lobster*

Arancia (l'arancia, le arance) for *orange*

Arancio (l'arancio, gli aranci) for *orange tree*

Arancione for *orange*

Arcipelago (l'arcipelago, gli arcipelaghi) for *archipelago*

Arco del piede for *arch*

Arcobaleno (l'arcobaleno, gli arcobaleni) for *rainbow*

Argento for *silver*

Arrabbiarsi for *to become angry*

Arrivare for *to arrive*

Arrivederci for *goodbye*

Arrivo (l'arrivo, gli arrivi) for *arrival*

Ascensore (l'ascensore, gli ascensori) for *elevator*

Asciugatrice (l'asciugatrice, le asciugatrici) for *dryer*

Ascoltare for *to listen*

Aspettare for *to wait*

Assai for *very much*

Assegno (l'assegno, gli assegni) for *check*

Assegno personale (l'assegno, gli assegni) for personal check

Assicurazione (l'assicurazione, le assicurazioni) for *insurance*

Assistente di volo (l'assistente, gli assistenti, le assistenti) for *flight attendant*

Atterraggio (l'atterraggio, gli atterraggi) for *landing*

Atterrare for *to land*

Attore (l'attore, gli attori) for *actor*

Attrice (l'attrice, le attrici) for *actress*

Auto (l'auto, le auto) for *car*

Autobus (l'autobus, gli autobus) for *bus*

Autolavaggio (l'autolavaggio, gli autolavaggi) *for car wash*

Automobile (l'automobile, le automobili) for *car*

Autonoleggio (l'autonoleggio, gli autonoleggi) for *car rental*

Autostrada (l'autostrada, le autostrade) for *highway*

Autunno (l'autunno, gli autunni) for *autumn*

Avaro (avaro, avari, avara, avare) for *stingy*

Avere for *to have*

Azzurro (azzurro, azzurri, azzurra, azzurre) for *light blue*

Babordo for *port*

Bagaglio (il bagaglio, i bagagli) for *baggage*

Bagaglio a mano (il bagaglio, i bagagli) for *Carry-on*

Bagno (il bagno, i bagni) for *bathroom*

Ballerine (la ballerina, le ballerine) for *ballet shoes*

Bambina (la bambina, le bambine) for *child (female)*

Bambino (il bambino, i bambini) for *child (male)*

Banana (la banana, le banane) for *banana*

Banca (la banca, le banche) for *bank*

Banco delle informazioni (il banco, i banchi) for *information desk*

Bancomat *for ATM or debit card*

Banconota (la banconota, le banconote) for *bill* or *banknote*

Bar (il bar, i bar) for *café*

Barca (la barca, le barche) for *boat*

Barca a remi (la barca, le barche) for *rowboat*

Barca a vela (la barca, le barche) for *sailboat*

Bastare *for to be enough*

Bastone (il bastone, i bastoni) for *cane*

Bella (bella, belle) for *beautiful*

Bellezza (la bellezza, le bellezze) for *beauty*

Bello (bello, belli) *for handsome*

Bene *for well*

Beneficiario (il beneficiario, i beneficiari) for *payee*

Benvenuto *for welcome*

Benzina (la benzina, le benzine) for *gas*

Bere for *to drink*

Berretto (il berretto, i berretti) for *cap*

Bianco (bianco, bianchi, bianca, bianche) for *white*

Bicchiere (il bicchiere, i bicchieri) for *glass*

Biglietteria (la biglietteria, le biglietterie) for *ticket booth or ticket office*

Biglietto (il biglietto, i biglietti) *for ticket*

Binario (il binario, i binari) for *track*

Biondo (biondo, biondi, bionda, bionde) for *blond*

Biscotti (il biscotto, i biscotti) for *cookie*

Bistecca (la bistecca, le bistecche) for *steak*

Blu for *dark blue*

Bocca (la bocca, le bocche) for *mouth*

Borsa (la borsa, le borse) for *bag or handbag*

Borsa a tracolla (la borsa, le borse) for *messenger bag*

Borsetta (la borsetta, le borsette) for *purse*

Bottone (il bottone, i bottoni) for *button*

Braccialetto (il braccialetto, i braccialetti) for *bracelet*

Braccio (il braccio, le braccia) for *arm*

Branzino (il branzino, i branzini) for *European Seabass*

Bravo (bravo, bravi, brava, brave) for *good, able*

Brina (la brina) for *frost*

Brodo (il brodo) for *broth*

Bruciarsi *for to get burned*

Brutto (brutto, brutti, brutta, brutte) for *ugly*

Bugiardo (bugiardo, bugiardi, bugiarda, bugiarde) for *liar*

Buono (buono, buoni, buona, buone) for *good*

Burrasca *(la burrasca, le burrasche)* for *storm*

Burro (il burro) for *butter*

Bus (il bus, i bus) for *bus*

Cabina (la cabina, le cabine) for *cabin*

Caffè (il caffè, i caffè) for *coffee*

Caffellatte (il caffellatte) for *caffellatte*

Calare *for to lower*

Caldo (caldo, caldi, calda, calde) for *warm*

Calmarsi for *to calm down*

Calmo (calmo, calmi, calma, calme) for *calm*

Calzini (il calzino, i calzini) for *socks*

Cambiavalute *(*il cambiavalute, i cambiavalute) for *currency exchange or bureau de exchange*

Cambiare *for to change*

Cambio for *exchange or exchange rate*

Camerino di prova (il camerino, i camerini) for *dressing room*

Camicetta (la camicetta, le camicette) for *blouse*

Camicia (la camicia, le camicie) for *button-down shirt*

Camminare for *to walk*

Campeggio (il campeggio, i campeggi) for *camping site*

Canale (il canale, i canali) for *canal*

Cane (il cane, i cani) for *dog*

Canottiera (la canottiera, le canottiere) for *undershirt*

Canzone (la canzone, le canzoni) for *song*

Capelli (i capelli) for *hair*

Capire for *to understand*

Capirsi *for to understand each other*

Capitano (il capitano, i capitani) for *captain*

Capodanno (il capodanno, i capodanni) for *New Year*

Cappello (il cappello, i cappelli) for *hat*

Cappotto (il cappotto, i cappotti) for *coat*

Cardigan (il cardigan, i cardigan) for *cardigan*

Carie (la carie, le carie) for *cavity*

Carino (carino, carini, carina, carine) for *nice*

Carne (la carne, le carni) *for meat*

Caro (caro, cari, cara, care) for *dear or expensive*

Carota (la carota, le carote) for *carrot*

Carrello (il carrello, i carrelli) for *cart*

Carro (il carro, i carri) for *wagon*

Carro attrezzi (il carro attrezzi, i carri attrezzi) for *tow truck*

Carta d'imbarco (la carta, le carte) for *boarding pass*

Carta da lettere (la carta, le carte) for *stationery*

Carta di credito (la carta, le carte) for *credit card*

Cartoleria (la cartoleria, le cartolerie) for *stationary store*

Cartolina (la cartolina, le cartoline) for *postcard*

Casa (la casa, le case) for *house*

Cassa (la cassa, le casse) for *register*

Cassetta delle lettere (la cassetta, le cassette) for *mailboxes*

Castello (il castello, i castelli) for *castle*

Catrame (il catrame) for *tar*

Cattivo (cattivo, cattivi, cattiva, cattive) for *bad*

Cavolfiore (il cavolfiore, i cavolfiori) for *cauliflower*

Cavolo (il cavolo, i cavoli) for *cabbage*

Celebrare for *to celebrate*

Cena (la cena, le cene) for *dinner*

Cenare for *to have dinner*

Centesimo (il centesimo, i centesimi) for *cent*

Centro commerciale (il centro commerciale, i centri commerciali) for *shopping mall*

Cercare for *to look for*

Cereali (i cereali) for *cereals*

Cerniera lampo (la cerniera, le cerniere) for *zipper*

Cerotti (il cerotto, i cerotti) for *Band-aid*

Certamente for *certainly*

Certo for *certain* or *sure* or *of course*

Cestino (il cestino, i cestini) for *basket*

Cetriolo (il cetriolo, i cetrioli) for *cucumber*

Che for *what* or *which*

Chi for *who*

Chiamarsi for *to be named, to be called*

Chiave (la chiave, le chiavi) for *key*

Chiedere for *to ask*

Chiedere in prestito for *to borrow*

Chiedersi for *to ask oneself*

Chilogrammo (il chilogrammo, i chilogrammi) for *kilogram*

Chilometro (il chilometro, i chilometri) for *kilometer*

Chitarra (la chitarra, le chitarre) for *guitar*

Chiudere *for to close*

Ciao for *hello or goodbye*

Cielo (il cielo, i cieli) for *sky*

Ciliegia (la ciliegia, le ciliegie) for *cherry*

Ciliegio (il ciliegio, i ciliegi) for *cherry tree*

Cina for *China*

Cinghiale (il cinghiale, i cinghiali) for *boar*

Cintura (la cintura, le cinture) for *belt*

Cintura di sicurezza (la cintura, le cinture) for *seatbelt*

Cioccolata (la cioccolata, le cioccolate) for *chocolate*

Cipolla (la cipolla, le cipolle) for *onion*

Cipria (la cipria) for *face powder*

Circa *for about*

Città (la città, le città) for *city*

Ciuccio (il ciuccio, i ciucci) for *pacifier*

Classe (la classe, le classi) for *class*

Cliente (il cliente, i clienti) for *client*

Clima (il clima, i climi) for *climate*

Colazione (la colazione, le colazioni) for *breakfast*

Collana (la collana, le collane) for *necklace*

Collant (il collant, i collant) for *tights, pantyhose*

Collo (il collo, i colli) for *neck*

Come *for how*

Commessa (la commessa, le commesse) for *shop assistant (female)*

Commesso (il commesso, i commessi) for *shop assistant (male)*

Commissione (la commissione, le commissioni) for *commission or fee*

Comò (il comò, i comò) for *chest of drawers*

Compagnia (la compagnia, le compagnie) for *company*

Comprare for *to buy*

Con *for* with

Condividere *for to share*

Condiviso (condiviso, condivisi, condivisa, condivise) for *shared*

Confermare for *to confirm*

Coniglio (il coniglio, i conigli, la coniglia, le coniglie) for *rabbit*

Conoscersi *for to know each other*

Contante (il contante) for *cash*

Conto corrente *(il conto, i conti)* for *checking account*

Conto (il conto, i conti) for *bill*

Contorni (il contorno, i contorni) *for side dishes*

Contro *for against*

Controllore (il controllore, i controllori) for *inspector*

Convento (il convento, i conventi) for *convent*

Coprifuoco (il coprifuoco, i coprifuochi) for *curfew*

Coprire for *to cover*

Cornetto (il cornetto, i cornetti) for *croissant*

Corto (corto, corti, corta, corte) for *short*

Cosa (la cosa, le cose) for *thing*

Cosa for *what*

Coscia (la coscia, le cosce) for *thigh*

Così così for *so and so*

Costare for *to cost*

Costoso (costoso, costosi, costosa, costose) for *expensive*

Cravatta (la cravatta, le cravatte) for *tie*

Credere for *to believe*

Crema (la crema, le creme) for *lotion*

Crema solare (la crema, le creme) for *sun lotion*

Crisi (la crisi, le crisi) for *crisis*

Crociera (la crociera, le crociere) for *cruise*

Cucina (la cucina, le cucine) *for kitchen*

Cuffia (la cuffia, le cuffie) *for headset*

Cugina (la cugina, le cugine) *for cousin, cousins (feminine)*

Cugino (il cugino, i cugini) for *cousin, cousins (masculine)*

Culla (la culla, le culle) for *bassinet*

Da *for from*

Dado (il dado, i dadi) for *dice*

Danno (il danno, i danni) for *damage*

Dappertutto *for everywhere*

Dare *for to give*

Darsena (la darsena, le darsene) for *harbor*

Davanti *for in front*

Debole (debole, deboli) for *weak*

Decagrammo *(il decagrammo, i decagrammi)* for *decagram*

Decollo (il decollo, i decolli) for *take off*

Degustazione (la degustazione, le degustazioni) for *tasting*

Delizioso (delizioso, deliziosi, deliziosa, deliziose) for *delicious*

Dente (il dente, i denti) for *tooth*

Dentifricio (il dentifricio, i dentifrici) for *totoothpaste*

Dentista (il dentista, i dentisti) for *dentist*

Dentro for *inside*

Destra *for right*

Detergente (il detergente, i detergenti) for *cleanser*

Detersivo (il detersivo, i detersivi) for *detergents*

Di for *of*

Di fronte for *in front of*

Di solito *for usually*

Dicembre *for December*

Dietro *for behind*

Difficile for *difficult*

Dilemma (il dilemma, i dilemmi) for *dilemma*

Diluviare for *to pour*

Dimenticarsi for *to get*

Dire for *to say*

Disgustoso (disgustoso, disgustosi, disgustosa, disgustose) for *disgusting*

Disinfettante (il disinfettante, i disinfettanti) for *disinfectant*

Dispiacere for *to regret*

Dita del piede for *toes*

Dito (il dito, le dita) for *finger*

Divertirsi for *to have fun*

Doccia (la doccia, le docce) for *shower*

Dolce for *sweet*

Dolcemente for *sweetly*

Dolci (il dolce, i dolci) for *dessert*

Dolere for *to suffer*

Dollaro (il dollaro, i dollari) for *dollar*

Domandare for *to ask*

Domandarsi for *to wonder*

Domani for *tomorrow*

Domenica for *Sunday*

Donna (la donna, le donne) for *woman*

Dopo for *after*

Doppio (doppio, doppi, doppia, doppie) for *double*

Dormire for *to sleep*

Dormitorio (il dormitorio, i dormitori) for *dorm*

Dottore (il dottore, i dottori) for *doctor*

Dottoressa (la dottoressa, le dottoresse) for *doctor (female)*

Dove for *where*

Dovere for *to have to*

Dovere for *to owe*

Dramma (il dramma, i drammi) for *drama*

Dritto for *straight*

Drogheria (la drogheria, le drogherie) for *drugstore*

Durante for *during*

Eccetto for *except*

Ecco for *here is and here are*

Economico (economico, economici, economica, economiche) for *convenient*

Elegante (elegante, eleganti) for *elegant*

Enoteca (l'enoteca, le enoteche) for *wine dealer*

Entrare for *to enter, to go in*

Epifania (l'Epifania) for *Epiphany*

Equipaggio (l'equipaggio, gli equipaggi) for *crew*

Esatto (esatto, esatti, esatta, esatte) for *exact*

Eseguire for *to carry out* or *to perform (on ATM machine instead of "enter")*

Essere for *to be*

Estate (l'estate, le estati) for *summer*

Ettogrammo (l'ettogrammo, gli ettogrammi) for *hectogram*

Faccia (la faccia, le facce) for *face*

Facile for *easy*

Facilmente for *easily*

Fagiolini (i fagiolini) for *green beans*

Famiglia (la famiglia, le famiglie) for *family*

Fantastico (fantastico, fantastici, fantastica, fantastiche) for *fantastic*

Fare for *to do*

Farmacia (la farmacia, le farmacie) for *pharmacy*

Farsi il bagno for *to take a bath*

Fato (il fato) for *fate*

Fatto (il fatto, i fatti) for *fact*

Fazzoletto di carta (il fazzoletto, i fazzoletti) for *tissue*

Febbraio *for February*

Febbre (la febbre, le febbri) for *fever*

Felice *for happy*

Felicemente *for happily*

Felpa (la felpa, le felpe) for *sweatshirt*

Fermata dell'autobus (la fermata, le fermate) for *the bus stop*

Fermo (fermo, fermi, ferma, ferme) for *still*

Festa (la festa, le feste) for *holiday*

Fetta (la fetta, le fette) for *slice*

Fettina (la fettina, le fettine) for *cutlet*

Fidarsi for *to trust*

Figlia (la figlia, le figlie) for *daughter*

Figlio (il figlio, i figli) for *son*

Fila (la fila, le file) for *line*

Film (il film, i film) for *movie*

Finire *for to finish*

Fino *for until*

Finora *for until now*

Fiore (il fiore, i fiori) for *flower*

Fiume (il fiume, i fiumi) for *river*

Foglio (il foglio, i fogli) *for sheet*

Fondotinta (il fondotinta, i fondotinta) for *foundation*

Formaggio (il formaggio, i formaggi) for *cheese*

Formale for *formal*

Fornaio (il fornaio, i fornai) for *bakery for bread and cookies*

Forte for *loudly, heavily*

Fortunatamente for *luckily*

Fortunato (fortunato, fortunati, fortunata, fortunate) for *lucky*

Foschia for *the haze, mist*

Foto (la foto, le foto) for *picture, photo*

Fragola *(la fragola, le fragole)* for *strawberry*

Franchigia (la franchigia, le franchigie) for *deductible*

Fratello (il fratello, i fratelli) for *brother, brothers*

Freddo (freddo, freddi, fredda, fredde) for *cold*

Frequente for *frequent*

Frequentemente for *frequently*

Frittelle (la frittella, le frittelle) for *pancakes*

Frutta (la frutta, i frutti) for *fruit*

Fruttivendolo (il fruttivendolo, i fruttivendoli) for *fruit and vegetable store*

Fungo (il fungo, i funghi) for *mushroom*

Fuori for *outside*

Gamba (la gamba, le gambe) for *leg*

Gambero (il gambero, i gamberi) for *prawn or shrimp*

Gatto (il gatto, i gatti, la gatta, le gatte) for *cat*

Gelateria (la gelateria, le gelaterie) for *ice cream parlor*

Gelato (il gelato, i gelati) for *ice cream*

Genero (il genero, i generi) for *son-in-law*

Generoso (generoso, generosi, generosa, generose) for *generous*

Gennaio for *January*

Gentile (gentile, gentili) for *kind*

Gentilmente for *kindly*

Ghetta (la ghetta, le ghette) for *gaiter*

Ghiaccio (il ghiaccio) for *ice*

Già for *already*

Giacca (la giacca, le giacche) for *jacket*

Giallo (giallo, gialli, gialla, gialle) for *yellow*

Giocare for *to play*

Gioco (il gioco, i giochi) for *game*

Gioielleria (la gioielleria, le gioiellerie) for *jewelry store*

Giornalaio (il giornalaio, i giornalai) for *newsstand*

Giornale (il giornale, i giornali) for *newspaper*

Giornaliero (giornaliero, giornalieri, giornaliera, giornaliere) for *daily*

Giorno (il giorno, i giorni) for *day*

Giovane (giovane, giovani) for *young*

Giovedì for *Thursday*

Girare for *to turn*

Girare un assegno for *to endorse*

Gita (la gita, le gite) for *trip*

Giù for *down, under*

Giubbotto (il giubbotto, i giubbotti) for *windbreaker*

Giubbotto di salvataggio (il giubbotto, i giubbotti) for *life jacket*

Giugno *for June*

Giusto (giusto, giusti, giusta, giuste) for *correct*

Glutine for *gluten*

Gnocchi (lo gnocco, gli gnocchi) for *gnocchi*

Gnomo (lo gnomo, gli gnomi) for *gnome*

Gola (la gola, le gole) for *throat*

Gondola (la gondola, le gondole) for *gondola*

Gonna (la gonna, le gonne) for *skirt*

Grammo (il grammo, i grammi) for *gram*

Grande (grande, grandi) for *big*

Grandi magazzini *for department store*

Grandinare for *to hail*

Grasso (grasso, grassi, grassa, grasse) for to *fat*

Grazie *for thank you*

Grigio (grigio, grigi, grigia, grigie) for *gray*

Guanto (il guanto, i guanti) for *glove*

Guardare *for to look*

Guardare le vetrine for *to go window shopping*

Guarito (guarito, guariti, guarita, guarite) for *healed*

Guidatore (il guidatore, i guidatori) for *driver*

Gusto (il gusto, i gusti) for *flavor*

Ieri for *yesterday*

Igiene *(l'igiene)* for *hygiene*

Illusione (l'illusione, le illusioni) for *the illusion*

Imbarcarsi for *to embark, to board*

Impermeabile (l'impermeabile, gli impermeabili) for *raincoat*

Impiegato for *clerk*

Importare for *to matter*

Importo (l'importo, gli importi) for *amount*

Improvviso for *sudden*

In for *in*

Incassare for *to cash*

Incluso *(incluso, inclusi, inclusa, incluse)* for *included*

Incontrarsi con for *to meet with*

Incrocio (l'incrocio, gli incroci) *for intersection*

Indicare *for to point*

Indietro for *behind, back*

Indipendente for *independent*

Indù for *hindu*

Informale for *casual*

Infradito (l'infradito) for *flip flops*

Insalata (l'insalata, le insalate) for *salad*

Interessare for *to interest*

Interesse (l'interesse, gli interessi) for *interest*

Interurbano for *suburban*

Intorno *for around*

Inverno (l'inverno, gli inverni) for *winter*

Inversione ad U for *U-turn*

Io for *I*

Ipocalorico *for low calories*

Ipocolesterolemico or *a basso contenuto di colesterolo* for *low cholesterol*

Iposodico for *low salt*

Ipotesi (l'ipotesi, le ipotesi) for *hypothesis*

Irritarsi for *to get irritated*

Isola (l'isola, le isole) for *island*

Isolato (l'isolato, gli isolati) for *block*

Issare for *to hoist*

Jeans (i jeans) for *jeans*

Kosher for *kosher*

Laggiù for *down there*

Lamentarsi di for *to complain about*

Lampo (il lampo, i lampi) for *lightning*

Lassù for *up there*

Latte (il latte) for *milk*

Lattosio for *lactose*

Lattuga (la lattuga) for *lettuce*

Lavanderia (la lavanderia, le lavanderie) *a gettoni* or *lavanderia automatica* for *laundromat*

Lavanderia (la lavanderia, le lavanderie) *a secco* for *dry cleaner*

Lavatrice (la lavatrice, le lavatrici) for *washing machine*

Lavorare for *to work*

Leggere for *to read*

Leggermente for *lightly*

Leggero (leggero, leggeri, leggera, leggere) for *light or bland*

Lei for *she*

Lento (lento, lenti, lenta, lente) for *slow*

Lentamente for *slowly*

Lente (la lente, le lenti) for *lens*

Lettera (la lettera, le lettere) for *letter*

Letto (il letto, i letti) for *bed*

Letto a castello (il letto a castello, i letti a castello) for *bunk bed*

Lezione (la lezione, le lezioni) for *lesson*

Lì in cima for *on top over there*

Lì in fondo for *down there*

Lì sopra for *up there*

Lì sotto for *down there*

Lì vicino for *over there*

Lì, là for *there*

Libreria (la libreria, le librerie) for *bookstore*

Libro (il libro, i libri) for *books*

Limone (il limone, i limoni) for *lemon*

Litro (il litro, i litri) for *liter*

Lontano for *far*

Loro, essi for *they*

Luglio for *July*

Lui for *he*

Lunedì for *Monday*

Lungo (lungo, lunghi, lunga, lunghe) for *long*

Macchina (la macchina, le macchine) for *car*

Macchina (la macchina, le macchine) *a noleggio* for *rental car*

Macelleria (la macelleria, le macellerie) for *butcher*

Macinata for *ground meat*

Madre (la madre, le madri) for *mother*

Maggio for *May*

Maglietta (la maglietta, le magliette) for *T-shirt*

Maglione (il maglione, i maglioni) for *sweater*

Magro (magro, magri, magra, magre) *for thin*

Mai for *never*

Maiale (il maiale, i maiali) for *pork*

Malato (malato, malati, malata, malate) for *sick*

Male for *badly*

Male for *bad*

Mancia *(la mancia, le mance)* for *tip*

Mangiare for *to eat*

Mano (la mano, le mani) for *hand*

Manzo for *beef*

Marcia (la marcia, le marce) for *gear*

Mare (il mare, i mari) for *sea*

Marinaio (il marinaio, i marinai) for *sailor*

Marito (il marito, i mariti) for *husband*

Marmellata (la marmellata, le marmellate) for *jam*

Marrone for *brown*

Martedì for *Tuesday*

Marzo for *March*

Mascara (il mascara, i mascara) for *mascara*

Matita (la matita, le matite) for *pencil*

Mattina (la mattina, le mattine) for *morning*

Mattino (il mattino, i mattini) for *morning*

Medio (medio, medi, media, medie) for *medium*

Meglio for *better*

Mela (la mela, le mele) for *apple*

Melo (il melo, i meli) for *apple tree*

Melone (il melone, i meloni) for *melon*

Membro (il membro, i membri) *for member*

Mensile for monthly

Menù for *menu*

Meraviglioso (meraviglioso, meravigliosi, meravigliosa, meravigliose) *for wonderful*

Mercoledì for *Wednesday*

Merenda (la merenda, le merende) for *snack*

Mese (il mese, i mesi) for *month*

Metro (il metro, i metri) for *meter*

Metropolitana (la metropolitana, le metropolitane) for *metro*

Mettersi for to put on

Mezzanotte (la mezzanotte) for *midnight*

Miele (il miele) for *honey*

Miglio (il miglio, le miglia) for *mile*

Minestra (la minestra, le minestre) for *soup*

Minimo (minimo, minimi, minima, minime) for *minimum*

Minuto (il minuto, i minuti) for *minutes*

Mirtillo (il mirtillo, i mirtilli) for *blueberry*

Mocassini (i mocassini) for *loafers*

Moglie (la moglie, le mogli) for *wife*

Molto for *much*

Monastero *(il monastero, i monasteri)* for *monastery*

Moneta *(la moneta, le monete)* for *coin*

Montagna *(la montagna, le montagne)* for *mountain*

Montatura *(la montatura, le montature)* for *frame*

Morire for *to die*

Motoscafo (il motoscafo, i motoscafi) for *motorboat*

Multa (la multa, le multe) for *fine*

Museo (il museo, i musei) for *museum*

Musulmano (musulmano, musulmani, musulmana, musulmane) for *muslim*

Mutande (la mutanda, le mutande) for *underwear*

Mutandina (la mutandina, le mutandine) for *panties*

Nascere for *to be born*

Natale for *Christmas*

Nave (la nave, le navi) *da crociera* for *cruise ship*

Nave (la nave, le navi) for *ship*

Nebbia (la nebbia, le nebbie) for *fog*

Negozio (il negozio, i negozi) for *store*

Negozio di alimentari (il negozio, i negozi) for *grocery store*

Negozio di abbigliamento (il negozio, i negozi) for *store for clothing*

Nero (nero, neri, nera, nere) for *black*

Neve (la neve, le nevi) for *snow*

Nevicare for *to snow*

Nipote (il nipote, i nipoti) for *nephew and grandson*

Nipote (la nipote, le nipoti) for *niece and granddaughter*

Noi for *we*

Noleggiare for *to rent*

Nonna (la nonna, le nonne) for *grandmother*

Nonno (il nonno, i nonni) for *grandfather*

Notte (la notte, le notti) for *night*

Novembre for *November*

Nuora (la nuora, le nuore) for *daughter-in-law*

Nuotare for *to swim*

Nuovo (nuovo, nuovi, nuova, nuove) for *new*

Nutrirsi for *to feed oneself*

Nuvola (la nuvola, le nuvole) for *cloud*

Nuvoloso for *overcast*

Obliterare for *to validate*

Occhio (l'occhio, gli occhi) for *eyes*

Offrire for *to offer*

Oggi for *day*

Ogni tanto for *every once in a while*

Olio (l'olio, gli olii) *for oil*

Oliva (l'oliva, le olive) for *olive*

Ombrello (l'ombrello, gli ombrelli) for *umbrella*

Onestamente for *honestly*

Onesto (onesto, onesti, onesta, oneste) for *honest*

Opera (l'opera, le opere) for *opera*

Ora for *now*

Orario (l'orario, gli orai) for *schedule*

Ordinare for *to order*

Orecchino (l'orecchino, gli orecchini) for *earrings*

Orecchio (l'orecchio, gli orecchi) for *ear*

Orologiaio (l'orologiaio, gli orologiai) for *watch seller*

Orologio (l'orologio, gli orologi) for *watch*

Ospedale (l'ospedale, gli ospedali) for *hospital*

Ospite (l'ospite, gli ospiti) for *guest*

Ostello (l'ostello, gli ostelli) for *hostel*

Ottobre for *October*

Overcraft for *hovercraft*

Ovunque for *everywhere*

Pacco (il pacco, i pacchi) for *package*

Padre (il padre, i padri) for *father*

Paese (il paese, i paesi) for *village or small town*

Pagamento (il pagamento, i pagamenti) for *payment*

Pagare for *to pay*

Paio (il paio, le paia) for *pair*

Palestra (la palestra, le palestre) for *gym*

Pane (il pane, i pani) for *bread*

Panetteria (la panetteria, le panetterie) for *bakery for bread and cookies*

Panificio (il panificio, i panifici) for *bakery for bread and cookies*

Panino (il panino, i panini) for *sandwich*

Panna (la panna) for *cream*

Pantaloncini (i pantaloncini) for *shorts*

Pantaloni (i pantaloni) for *trousers*

Pantofole (la pantofola, le pantofole) for *slippers*

Papà (il papà, i papà) for *dad*

Papa *(il Papa, i Papi)* for *pope*

Parcheggio (il parcheggio, i parcheggi) *dei taxi* for *taxi rank*

Parlare *for to speak*

Parlarsi *for to talk to each other*

Partenza (la partenza, le partenze) for *departure*

Partire *for to leave*

Pasqua for *Easter*

Passaporto for *passport*

Passeggero (il passeggero, i passeggeri) for *passenger*

Passeggero a piedi *for foot passenger*

Passerella for *gangway*

Pasto (il pasto, i pasti) for *meal*

Pasticceria (la pasticceria, le pasticcerie) for *bakery for pastry*

Patata (la patata, le patate) for *potato*

Pausa (la pausa, le pause) for *break*

Pedaggio (il pedaggio, i pedaggi) for *toll*

Pellegrina (la pellegrina, le pellegrine) for (female) *pilgrim*

Pellegrino (il pellegrino, i pellegrini) for (male) *pilgrim*

Penisola (la penisola, le penisole) for *peninsula*

Penna (la penna, le penne) for *pen*

Pensilina (la pensilina, le pensiline) for *platform*

Pensione (la pensione, le pensioni) for *small hotel*

Per *for in order to*

Pera (la pera, le pere) for *pear*

Percentuale (la percentuale, le percentuali) for *the percentage*

Perché *for why, because*

Perdere for *to lose*

Permanente (la permanente, le permanenti) for *perm*

Pero (il pero, i peri) for *pear tree*

Personale for *personal*

Pesca (la pesca, le pesche) for *peach*

Pesce (il pesce, i pesci) for *fish*

Pescheria (la pescherie, le pescherie) for *the fish market*

Pesco (il pesco, i peschi) for *peach tree*

Pettine (il pettine, i pettini) for *comb*

Petto (il petto, i petti) for *breast*

Piacere *for pleasure*

Piacere for *to like*

Piangere for *to cry*

Piano for *slowly, quietly*

Piazza (la piazza, le piazze) for *square*

Piccolo (piccolo, piccoli, piccola, piccole) for *small*

Piede (il piede, i piedi) for *foot*

Pilota (il pilota, i piloti) for *pilot*

Pioggia (la pioggia) for *rain*

Piombatura (la piombatura, le piombature) for *filling*

Piovere for *to rain*

Piscina (la piscina, le piscine) for *pool*

Pisello (il pisello, i piselli) for *pea*

Pisolino (il pisolino, i pisolini) for *nap*

Pittore (il pittore, i pittori) *for painter*

Più tardi for *later*

Pizza for *pizza*

Plastic (la plastica, le plastiche) for *plastic*

Platino for *platinum*

Poco for *some, a little*

Poi for *then*

Pollo (il pollo, i polli) for *chicken*

Polipo (il polipo, i polipi) for *Octopus*

Polso (il polso, i polsi) for *wrist*

Pomeriggio (il pomeriggio, i pomeriggi) for *afternoon*

Pomodoro (il pomodoro, i pomodori) for *tomato*

Pompa (la pompa, le pompe) for *pump*

Pompelmo (il pompelmo, i pompelmi) for *grapefruit*

Ponte *(il ponte, i ponti)* for *bridge or deck*

Porcile (il porcile, i porcili) for *pig pen*

Porto (il porto, i porti) for *port*

Posto (il posto, i posti) for *seat*

Potere for *to be able to*

Povero *(*povero, poveri, povera, povere) for *poor*

Pranzare for *to have lunch*

Pranzo (il pranzo, i pranzi) for *lunch*

Preghiera (la preghiera, le preghiere) for *prayer*

Prego for *you are welcome*

Prelievo (il prelievo, i prelievi) for *withdrawal*

Prenotare for *to reserve*

Preoccuparsi for *to worry*

Prepararsi for *to get ready*

Presentarsi for *to introduce oneself*

Prestare for *to lend*

Prestito (il prestito, i prestiti) for *loan*

Presto for *soon or early*

Prezzo (il prezzo, i prezzi) for *price*

Prima for *before*

Primavera (la primavera, le primavere) for *spring*

Prosciutto cotto (il prosciutto, i prosciutti) for *ham*

Prosciutto crudo (il prosciutto, i prosciutti) for *prosciutto*

Prodotto (il prodotto, i prodotti) for *product*

Professore (il professore, i professori) for *professor*

Professoressa (la professoressa, le professoresse) for *professor (female)*

Profumato (profumato, profumati, profumata, profumate) for *fragrant*

Profumeria (la profumeria, le profumerie) for *perfume store*

Programma (il programma, i programmi) for *program*

Pronto soccorso for *emergency room*

Proseguire for *to continue*

Prossimo (prossimo, prossimi, prossima, prossime) for *next*

Provare for *to try on*

Provvisoriamente for *temporarily*

Provvisorio for *temporary*

Prua for *bow*

Psicologo (lo psicologo, gli psicologi) for *psychologist*

Pulito (pulito, puliti, pulita, pulite) for *clean*

Quaggiù for *down here*

Quale for *which*

Quando for *When*

Quanto for *how much*

Quassù for *up here*

Quello (quello, quelli, quella, quelle) for *that*

Questo (questo, questi, questa, queste) for *this*

Qui, qua for *here*

Radio (la radio, le radio) for *radio*

Raffreddore (il raffreddore, i raffreddori) *for cold*

Ragazza (la ragazza, le ragazze) *for girl*

Ragazzo (il ragazzo, i ragazzi) for *boy*

Rallegrarsi for *to rejoice*

Raramente for *rarely*

Recente for *recent*

Reggiseno (il reggiseno, i reggiseni) for *bra*

Regina (la regina, le regine) for *queen*

Regola (la regola, le regole) for *rule*

Resto (il resto) for *change*

Ricco (ricco, ricchi, ricca, ricche) for *rich*

Ricevuta (la ricevuta, le ricevute) for *receipt*

Rimborsare for *to refund*

Rimborso (il rimborso, i rimborsi) for *refund*

Riparare for *to fix*

Riparazione (la riparazione, le riparazioni) for *repair*

Ripetere *for to repeat*

Riposare for *to rest*

Riposarsi for *to rest*

Riposato (riposato, riposati, riposata, riposate) for *rested*

Risotto (il risotto, i risotti) for *rice dish*

Risparmiare for *to save*

Rispondere *for to answer*

Ristorante (il ristorante, i ristoranti) for *restaurant*

Ritardo for *delay*

Rompere *for to break*

Rosa for *pink*

Rossetto (il rossetto, i rossetti) for *lipstick*

Rosso (rosso, rossi, rossa, rosse) for *red*

Rotatoria (la rotatoria, le rotatorie) for *rotary*

Rugiada *for dew*

Sabato for *Saturday*

Salame *(il salame, i salami) for salami*

Saldo *for balance*

Sale (il sale, i sali) for *salt*

Salire for *to go up*

Salmone (il salmone, i salmoni) for *salmon*

Salotto (il salotto, i salotti) for *living room*

Salpare for *to sail*

Salumeria (la salumeria, le salumerie) for *cold cuts, cheese, olives*

Salvagente *(il salvagente, i salvagente) for life belt*

Salve for *hello*

Sandali (il sandalo, i sandali) for *sandals*

Sapere *for to know*

Sbarcare for *to disembark*

Scarpa (la scarpa, le scarpe) for *shoe*

Scarpe da ginnastica (la scarpa, le scarpe) *for sneakers*

Scatoletta (la scatoletta, le scatolette) for *can*

Scatto (lo scatto, gli scatti) for *click*

Scena (la scena, le scene) for *scene*

Scendere *for to go down*

Scherzo (lo scherzo, gli scherzi) for *joke*

Schiaffo (lo schiaffo, gli schiaffi) for *slap*

Schienale (lo schienali, gli schienali) for *seat-back*

Sci (gli sci) for *ski*

Scialle (lo scialle, gli scialli) for *shawl*

Scialuppa di salvataggio (la scialuppa, le scialuppe) for *lifeboat*

Sciarpa (la sciarpa, le sciarpe) for *scarf*

Sciocco (sciocco, sciocchi, sciocca, sciocche) for *silly*

Sciupato (sciupato, sciupati, sciupata, sciupate) for *damaged, spoil*

Scoprire for *to discover*

Scossa (la scossa, le scosse) for *shake, [electric] shock*

Scrittore (lo scrittore, gli scrittori) *for writer (male)*

Scrittrice (la scrittrice, le scrittrici) for *writer (female)*

Scrivere *for to write*

Scriversi *for to write to each other*

Scultore (lo scultore, gli scultori) for *sculptor*

Scultrice (la scultrice, le scultrici) for *sculptress*

Scuola (la scuola, le scuole) for *school*

Scuro (scuro, scuri, scura, scure) for *dark*

Scusarsi for *to apologize*

Sedano (il sedano, i sedani) for *celery*

Sedersi for *to sit*

Sedile (il sedile, i sedili) *for seat*

Seggiolino (il seggiolino, i seggiolini) for *car seat*

Seguire *for to follow*

Selvaggina (la selvaggina) for *game*

Semaforo (il semaforo, i semafori) for *traffic light*

Sembrare for *to seem*

Sempre *for always*

Sentire *for to hear*

Senza for *without*

Sera *(la sera, le sere) for evening*

Servire for *to serve*

Servire *for to need*

Settembre for *September*

Settimana (la settimana, le settimane) for *week*

Settimanale for *weekly*

Shuttle for *shuttle*

Sicurezza *for security*

Signora for *Mrs*

Signore for *Mr*

Signori *for Mr and Mrs*

Signorina for *signorina*

Silenziosamente for *quietly*

Silenzioso (silenzioso, silenziosi, silenziosa, silenziose) for *quiet*

Sincero (sincero, sinceri, sincera, sincere) for *sincere*

Singolo (singolo, singoli, singola, singole) for *single*

Sinistra *for left*

Sistema (il sistema, i sistemi) for *system*

Smalto (lo smalto, gli smalti) for *nail polish*

Smog (lo smog, gli smog) for *smog*

Sogno (il sogno, i sogni) for *dream*

Soldi (il soldo, i soldi) for *money*

Sole (il sole) for *sun*

Sopra *for on, above*

Sorella (la sorella, le sorelle) for *sister*

Sotto for *under, below*

Sottoveste (la sottoveste, le sottovesti) for *slip*

Sovrapprezzo (il sovrapprezzo, i sovrapprezzi) for *surcharge*

Spada (pesce spada) for *swordfish*

Spaventarsi for *to get frightened*

Spazzola (la spazzola, le spazzole) for *brush*

Spazzolarsi for *brush (teeth or hair)*

Spazzolino da denti (lo spazzolino, gli spazzolini) for *toothbrush*

Spegnere for *to turn off*

Spendere for *to spend*

Spesa (la spesa) for *grocery shopping*

Spese (le spese) for *shopping*

Spezia (la spezia, le spezie) for *spice*

Spiaggia (la spiaggia, le spiagge) for *beach*

Spilla (la spilla, le spille) for *brooch*

Spinaci (lo spinacio, gli spinaci) for *spinach*

Sporco (sporco, sporchi, sporca, sporche) for *dirty*

Sport (lo sport, gli sport) for *sport*

Sportivo for *casual*

Stadio (lo stadio, gli stadi) for *stadium*

Stagione (la stagione, le stagioni) for *season*

Stancante (stancante, stancanti) for *tiring*

Stanco (stanco, stanchi, stanca, stanche) for *tired*

Stanza (la stanza, le stanze) for *room*

Stare for *to be, to stay*

Statua (la statua, le statue) for *statue*

Stazione (la stazione, le stazioni) for *station*

Stazione (la stazione, le stazioni) **di polizia** for *the police station*

Stazione (la stazione, le stazioni) **di servizio** for *service station*

Stella (la stella, le stelle) for *star*

Stipendio (lo stipendio, gli stipendi) for *salary*

Stivali (lo stivale, gli stivali) for *boots*

Stomaco (lo stomaco, gli stomaci) for *stomach*

Strada (la strada, le strade) for *road*

Su for *up, on*

Suocera (la suocera, le suocere) for *mother-in-law*

Suocero (il suocero, i suoceri) for *father-in-law*

Supermercato (il supermercato, i supermercati) for *supermarket*

Superstrada (la superstrada, le superstrade) for *expressway*

Susina (la susina, le susine) for *plum*

Svegliarsi for *to wake oneself up*

Svestirsi for *to get undressed*

Tabaccheria (la tabaccheria, le tabaccherie) for *tobacco shop*

Tacchino (il tacchino, i tacchini) for *turkey*

Tacco (il tacco, i tacchi) for *heel (of the shoe)*

Taglia (la taglia, le taglie) for *size*

Taglio di capelli for *haircut*

Tallone (il tallone, i talloni) for *heel (of the foot)*

Tanto for *so much, a lot*

Tardi for *late*

Tartaruga (la tartaruga, le tartarughe) for *turtle*

Tasca (la tasca, le tasche) for *pocket*

Tassa (la tassa, le tasse) for *fee*

Tasso d'interesse for *interest rate*

Tavolo (il tavolo, i tavoli) for *table*

Taxi (il taxi, i taxi) for *cab*

Tazza (la tazza, le tazze) for *cup*

Tazzina (la tazzina, le tazzine) for *small cup*

Tè (il tè) for *tea*

Teatro (il teatro, i teatri) for *theater*

Temperatura (la temperatura, le temperature) for *temperature*

Tempo (il tempo, i tempi) for *time, weather*

Temporale (il temporale, i temporali) for *storm*

Tenere for *to keep*

Testa (la testa, le teste) for *head*

Timone (il timone, i timoni) for *helm*

Togliersi for *to take off*

Tonno (il tonno, i tonni) for *tuna*

Tornare for *to return*

Tra or ***fra*** for *among, in between*

Traghetto (il traghetto, i traghetti) for *ferry*

Tranne for *except*

Trasferire for *to transfer*

Trasporto for *transportation*

Travellers cheque *for traveler's checks*

Traversata (la traversata, le traversate) for *crossing*

Treno (il treno, i treni) for *train*

Tribordo for *starboard*

Tristemente for *sadly*

Troppo for *too much*

Trota (la trota, le trote) for *trout*

Truccarsi *for to put on makeup*

Trucco (il trucco, i trucchi) for *makeup*

Tu *for you*

Tuono (il tuono, i tuoni) for *thunder*

Turbolenza (la turbolenza, le turbolenze) for *turbulence*

Tutto (tutto, tutti, tutta, tutte) for *all*

Ultimamente for *lastly*

Ultimo (ultimo, ultimi, ultima, ultime) *for last*

Umido (umido, umidi, umida, umide) for *humid*

Uomo (l'uomo, gli uomini) for *man*

Uova fritte *for fried eggs*

Uova sode for *hardboiled eggs*

Uova strapazzate *for scrambled eggs*

Uovo (l'uovo, le uova) for *egg*

Urbano for *urban*

Uscire *for to go out*

Uscite di emergenza for *emergency exits*

Uva (l'uva) for *grapes*

Vaglia postale *for money order*

Valigia (la valigia, le valigie) for *suitcase*

Valle (la valle, le valli) for *valley*

Valuta (la valuta, le valute) for *currency*

Vaporetto (il vaporetto, i vaporetti) for *steamboat*

Vassoio (il vassoio, i vassoi) for *tray*

Vecchio (vecchio, vecchi, vecchia, vecchie) *for old*

Vedersi *for to see each other*

Vegano for *vegan*

Vegetariano for *vegetarian*

Vela (la vela, le vele) for *sail*

Veliero for *sailing ship*

Vendere *for to sell*

Vendita for *sale*

Venerdì for *Friday*

Venire for *to come*

Vento (il vento, i venti) for *wind*

Verde *for green*

Verdura (la verdura, le verdure) for *vegetable*

Verdure al forno for *baked vegetables*

Verdure grigliate *for grilled vegetables*

Versamento *(il versamento, i versamenti) for deposit*

Vestire for *to dress*

Vestirsi *for to get dressed*

Vestito (il vestito, i vestiti) for *dress*

Vetrina (la vetrina, le vetrine) for *window*

Via *for away*

Via (la via, le vie) for *street*

Viaggiatore (il viaggiatore, i viaggiatori) for *traveler*

Vicino for *near, close*

Vigile urbano for *traffic policeman*

Vigna (la vigna, le vigne) for *vineyard*

Villa (la villa, le ville) for *villa*

Vino (il vino, i vini) for *wine*

Viola for *purple*

Vivere for *to live*

Voi *for you (many)*

Volare for *to fly*

Volere *for to want*

Voltare for *to turn*

Vomitare for *to vomit*

Yogurt (lo yogurt, gli yogurt) for *yogurt*

Zaino (lo zaino, gli zaini) for *backpack*

Zattera (la zattera, le zattere) for *raft*

Zia (la zia, le zie) for *aunt*

Zio (lo zio, gli zii) for *uncle*

Zitto (zitto, zitti, zitta, zitte) for *quiet*

Zone (la zona, le zone) for *zone*

Zucca (la zucca, le zucche) for *pumpkin*

Zucchero (lo zucchero) for *sugar*

Zuppa (la zuppa, le zuppe) for *soup*

English – Italian

at, to for *A*

about *for Circa*

actor for *Attore (l'attore, gli attori)*

actress for *Attrice (l'attrice, le attrici)*

after for *Dopo*

afternoon for *Pomeriggio (il pomeriggio, i pomeriggi)*

against *for Contro*

agency for *Agenzia (l'agenzia, le agenzie)*

airplane for *Aeroplano (l'aeroplano, gli aeroplani)*

airport for *Aeroporto (l'aeroporto, gli aeroporti)*

a little *for Poco*

all for *Tutto (tutto, tutti, tutta, tutte)*

already *for Già*

always for *Sempre*

amount for *Importo (l'importo, gli importi)*

analysis for *Analisi (l'analisi, le analisi)*

animal for *Animale (l'animale, gli animali)*

answer for *Rispondere*

anus *for Ano (l'ano, gli ani)*

aperitif for *Aperitivo (l'aperitivo, gli aperitivi)*

apologize *for Scusarsi*

appetizer for *Antipasto (l'antipasto, gli antipasti)*

apple for *Mela (la mela, le mele)*

apple tree for *Melo (il melo, i meli)*

apricot for *Albicocca (l'albicocca, le albicocche)*

April *for Aprile*

aquarium for *Acquario (l'acquario, gli acquari)*

arch for *Arco del piede*

archipelago for *Arcipelago (l'arcipelago, gli arcipelaghi)*

arm for *Braccio (il braccio, le braccia)*

around for *Intorno*

arrival for *Arrivo (l'arrivo, gli arrivi)*

arrive *(to)* for *Arrivare*

as soon as possible *for Appena*

ask *(to)* for *Chiedere*

ask *(to)* for *Domandare*

ask oneself *(to) for Chiedersi*

assistant *(male)* for *Commesso (il commesso, i commessi)*

ATM *or* **debit card** *for Bancomat*

August for *Agosto*

aunt for *Zia (la zia, le zie)*

autumn for *Autunno (l'autunno, gli autunni)*

away *for Via*

backpack for *Zaino (lo zaino, gli zaini)*

bad for *Cattivo (cattivo, cattivi, cattiva, cattive)*

bad for *Male*

badly *for Male*

bag *or* **handbag** *for Borsa (la borsa, le borse)*

baggage for *Bagaglio (il bagaglio, i bagagli)*

bakery for *bread and cookies Fornaio (il fornaio, i fornai)*

bakery *for bread and cookies Panetteria (la panetteria, le panetterie)*

bakery for *bread and cookies Panificio (il panificio, i panifici)*

bakery for *pastry Pasticceria (la pasticceria, le pasticcerie)*

balance *for Saldo*

ballet shoes for *Ballerine (la ballerina, le ballerine)*

banana for *Banana (la banana, le banane)*

Band-aid for *Cerotti (il cerotto, i cerotti)*

bank for *Banca (la banca, le banche)*

banknote for *Banconota (la banconota, le banconote)*

basket for *Cestino (il cestino, i cestini)*

bassinet for *Culla (la culla, le culle)*

bathroom for *Bagno (il bagno, i bagni)*

be able *(to) for Potere*

be *(to) for Essere*

be named *(to), be called (to) for Chiamarsi*

beach for *Spiaggia (la spiaggia, le spiagge)*

beautiful *for Bella (bella, belle)*

beauty for *Bellezza (la bellezza, le bellezze)*

because *for Perché*

become angry *(to)* for *Arrabbiarsi*

bed for *Letto (il letto, i letti)*

before *for Prima*

beef for *Manzo*

behind for *Dietro*

behind, back for *Indietro*

believe *(to) for Credere*

belt for *Cintura (la cintura, le cinture)*

better for *Meglio*

between *for Tra or fra*

big *for Grande (grande, grandi)*

bill for *Conto (il conto, i conti)*

black for *Nero (nero, neri, nera, nere)*

block for *Isolato (l'isolato, gli isolati)*

blond for *Biondo (biondo, biondi, bionda, bionde)*

blouse for *Camicetta (la camicetta, le camicette)*

blueberry for *Mirtillo (il mirtillo, i mirtilli)*

boar for *Cinghiale (il cinghiale, i cinghiali)*

board *(to)* for *Imbarcarsi*

boarding pass *for Carta d'imbarco (la carta, le carte)*

boat for *Barca (la barca, le barche)*

bookstore for *Libreria (la libreria, le librerie)*

book for *Libro (il libro, i libri)*

boots for *Stivali (lo stivale, gli stivali)*

borrow *(to) for Chiedere in prestito*

bow *for Prua*

boy for *Ragazzo (il ragazzo i ragazzi)*

bra for *Reggiseno (il reggiseno, i reggiseni)*

---

bracelet for *Braccialetto (il braccialetto, i braccialetti)*

bread for *Pane (il pane, i pani)*

break for *Pausa (la pausa, le pause)*

break *(to) for Rompere*

breakfast for *Colazione (la colazione, le colazioni)*

breast for *Petto (il petto, i petti)*

bridge for *Ponte (il ponte, i ponti)*

brooch for *Spilla (la spilla, le spille)*

broth for *Brodo (il brodo)*

brother for *Fratello (il fratello, i fratelli)*

brown *for Marrone*

brush *(teeth or hair) (to) for Spazzolarsi*

brush for *Spazzola (la spazzola, le spazzole)*

bunk bed for *Letto a castello (il letto a castello, i letti a castello)*

bus for *Bus (il bus, i bus)*

bus stop for *Fermata dell'autobus (la fermata, le fermate)*

busses for *Autobus (l'autobus, gli autobus)*

butcher for *Macelleria (la macelleria, le macellerie)*

butter for *Burro (il burro)*

button for *Bottone (il bottone, i bottoni)*

button-down shirt for *Camicia (la camicia, le camicie)*

buy *(to) for Comprare*

cab for *Taxi (il taxi, i taxi)*

cabbage for *Cavolo (il cavolo, i cavoli)*

cabin for *Cabina (la cabina, le cabine)*

café for *Bar (il bar, i bar)*

cafe latte *(coffee with milk)* for *Caffelatte (il caffelatte)*

calm for *Calmo (calmo, calmi, calma, calme)*

calm down *(to) for Calmarsi*

camping site for *Campeggio (il campeggio, campeggi)*

can for *Scatoletta (la scatoletta, le scatolette)*

canal for *Canale (il canale, i canali)*

cancel *(to)* for *Annullare*

cane for *Bastone (il bastone, i bastoni)*

cap for *Berretto (il berretto, i berretti)*

captain for *Capitano (il capitano, i capitani)*

car for *Auto (l'auto, le auto)*

car for *Automobile (l'automobile, le automobili)*

car for *Macchina (la macchina, le macchine)*

car (rental) for *Autonoleggio (l'autonoleggio, gli autonoleggi)*

car seat for *Seggiolino (il sedile, i sedili)*

car wash for *Autolavaggio (l'autolavaggio, gli autolavaggi)*

cardigan for *Cardigan (il cardigan, i cardigan)*

carrot for *Carota (la carota, le carote)*

Carry-on for *Bagaglio a mano (il bagaglio, i bagagli)*

cart for *Carrello (il carrello, i carrelli)*

cash for *Contante (il contante)*

cash *(to)* for *Incassare*

castle for *Castello (il castello, i castelli)*

casual for *Informale*

---

casual for Sportivo

cat for *Gatto (il gatto, i gatti, la gatta, le gatte)*

cauliflower for *Cavolfiore (il cavolfiore, i cavolfiori)*

cavity for *Carie (la carie, le carie)*

celebrate (to) for *Celebrare*

celery for *Sedano (il sedano)*

cents for *Centesimo (il centesimo, i centesimi)*

cereal for *Cereali (i cereali)*

certain for *Certo*

certainly for Certamente

change (to) for *Cambiare*

change for *Resto (il resto)*

check for *Assegno (l'assegno, gli assegni)*

checking account for *Conto corrente (il conto, i conti)*

cheese for *formaggio (il formaggio, i formaggi)*

cherry for *Ciliegia (la ciliegia, le ciliegie)*

cherry tree for *Ciliegio (il ciliegio, i ciliegi)*

chest of drawers for Comò (il comò, i comò)

chicken for *Pollo (il pollo, i polli)*

child (female) for *Bambina (la bambina, le bambine)*

child (male) for *Bambino (il bambino, i bambini)*

China for *Cina*

chocolate for *Cioccolata (la cioccolata, le cioccolate)*

Christmas for *Natale*

city for Città (la città, le città)

class for *Classe (la classe, le classi)*

clean for *Pulito (pulito, puliti, pulita, pulite)*

cleanser for *Detergente (il detergente, i detergenti)*

clerk for *Addetto (l'addetto, gli addetti)*

clerk for *Impiegato*

click for *Scatto (lo scatto, gli scatti)*

client for *Cliente (il cliente, i clienti)*

climate for *Clima (il clima, i climi)*

close for *Chiudere*

cloud for *Nuvola (la nuvola, le nuvole)*

coat for *Cappotto (il cappotto, i cappotti)*

coffee *for Caffè (il caffè, i caffè)*

coin for *Moneta (la moneta, le monete)*

cold cuts store for *Salumeria (la salumeria, le salumerie)*

cold for *Freddo (freddo, freddi, fredda, fredde)*

cold for *Raffreddore (il raffreddore, i raffreddori)*

comb for *Pettine (il pettine, i pettini)*

come *(to)* for *Venire*

commission or *fee* for *Commissione (la commissione, le commissioni)*

company for *Compagnia (la compagnia, le compagnie)*

complain about *(to) for Lamentarsi di*

confirm *(to)* for *Confermare*

continue *(to)* for *Proseguire*

convenient for *Economico (economico, economici, economica, economiche)*

---

convent for *Convento (il convento, i conventi)*

cookies for *Biscotti (il biscotto, i biscotti)*

correct for *Giusto (giusto, giusti, giusta, giuste)*

cost *(to)* for *Costare*

cousin *(feminine)* for *Cugina (la cugina, le cugine)*

cousin *(masculine)* for *Cugino (il cugino, i cugini)*

cover *(to)* for *Coprire*

cream for *Panna (la panna)*

credit card for *Carta di credito (la carta, le carte)*

crew for *Equipaggio (l'equipaggio, gli equipaggi)*

crisis for *Crisi (la crisi, le crisi)*

croissant for *Cornetto (il cornetto, i cornetti)*

crossing for *Traversata*

cruise for *Crociera (la crociera, le crociere)*

cruise ship for *Nave (la nave, le navi) da crociera*

cry *(to)* for *Piangere*

cucumber for *Cetriolo (il cetriolo, i cetrioli)*

cup for *Tazza (la tazza, le tazze)*

(small) cup for *Tazzina (la tazzina, le tazzine)*

curfew for *Coprifuoco (il coprifuoco, i coprifuochi)*

currency exchange or *bureau de change* for *Cambiavalute (il cambiavalute, i cambiavalute)*

currency for *Valuta (la valuta, le valute)*

cutlet for *Fettina (la fettina, le fettine)*

dad for *Papà (il papà, i papà)*

daily for *Giornaliero (giornaliero, giornalieri, giornaliera, giornaliere)*

damage for *Danno (il danno, i danni)*

damaged for *Sciupato (sciupato, sciupati, sciupata, sciupate)*

dark blue for *Blu*

dark for *Scuro (scuro, scuri, scura, scure)*

daughter for *Figlia (la figlia, le figlie)*

daughter-in-law for *Nuora (la nuora, le nuore)*

day for *Giorno (il giorno, i giorni)*

dear for *Caro (caro, cari, cara, care)*

December for *Dicembre*

deck for *Ponte (il ponte, i ponti)*

deductible for *Franchigia (la franchigia, le franchigie)*

decagrams *for Decagrammo*

delicious for *Delizioso (delizioso, deliziosi, deliziosa, deliziose)*

dentist for *Dentifricio (il dentifricio, i dentifrici)*

dentist for *Dentista (il dentista, i dentisti)*

department store for *Grandi magazzini*

departure for *Partenza (la partenza, le partenze)*

deposit for *Versamento (il versamento, i versamenti)*

dessert for *Dolce (il dolce, i dolci)*

detergent for *Detersivo (il detersivo, i detersivi)*

dew *for Rugiada*

dice for *Dado (il dado, i dadi)*

die *(to)* for *Morire*

difficult *for Difficile*

dilemma for *Dilemma (il dilemma, i dilemmi)*

dinner for *Cena (la cena, le cene)*

dirty for *Sporco (sporco, sporchi, sporca, sporche)*

discover *(to)* for *Scoprire*

disembark *(to)* for *Sbarcare*

disgusting for *Disgustoso (disgustoso, disgustosi, disgustosa, disgustose)*

disinfectant for *Disinfettante (il disinfettante, i disinfettanti)*

do *(to) for Fare*

doctor *(female)* for *Dottoressa (la dottoressa, le dottoresse)*

doctor *(male)* for *Dottore (il dottore, i dottori)*

dog for *Cane (il cane, i cani)*

dollar for *Dollaro (il dollaro, i dollari)*

dorm for *Dormitorio (il dormitorio, i dormitori)*

double for *Doppio (doppio, doppi, doppia, doppie)*

down here *for Quaggiù*

down there *for Laggiù*

down there *for Lì in fondo*

down there *for Lì sotto*

down, under *for Giù*

drama for *Dramma (il dramma, i drammi)*

dream for *Sogno (il sogno, i sogni)*

dress *(to)* for *Vestire*

dress for *Vestito (il vestito, i vestiti)*

---

dressing room for *Camerino di prova (il camerino, i camerini)*

drink *(to)* for *Bere*

driver for *Guidatore (il guidatore, i guidatori)*

drugstore for *Drogheria (la drogheria, le drogherie)*

dry cleaner for *Lavanderia (la lavanderia, le lavanderie) a secco*

dryer for *Asciugatrice (l'asciugatrice, le asciugatrici)*

during *for Durante*

ear for *Orecchio (l'orecchio, gli orecchi)*

earrings for *Orecchino (l'orecchino, gli orecchini)*

easily *for Facilmente*

Easter *for Pasqua*

easy *for Facile*

eat *(to)* for *Mangiare*

egg for *Uovo (l'uovo, le uova)*

eggs *(fried)* for *Uova fritte*

eggs *(hardboiled)* for *Uova sode*

eggs *(scrambled)* for *Uova strapazzate*

elegant for *Elegante (elegante, eleganti)*

elevator for *Ascensore (l'ascensore, gli ascensori)*

emergency for *emergenza (l'emergenza, le emergenze)*

emergency exits for *Uscite di emergenza*

emergency room for *Pronto soccorso*

endorse *(to)* for *Girare [un assegno]*

enough for *Abbastanza*

enough *(to be) for Bastare*

enter (to) for *inserire or digitare*

enter (to), go in (to) for Entrare

epiphany for *Epifania (l'Epifania)*

evening for *Sera (la sera, le sere)*

every once in a while for Ogni tanto

everywhere for Dappertutto

everywhere for Ovunque

exact for *Esatto (esatto, esatti, esatta, esatte)*

except for *Eccetto*

except for Tranne

exchange rate for Tasso di cambio

expensive for *Caro (caro, cari, cara, care)*

expensive for *Costoso (costoso, costosi, costosa, costose)*

expressway for *Superstrada (la superstrada, le superstrade)*

eye for *Occhio (l'occhio, gli occhi)*

face for *Faccia (la faccia, le facce)*

face powder for *Cipria (la cipria)*

fact for *Fatto (il fatto, i fatti)*

fall asleep (to) for *Addormentarsi*

family for *Famiglia (la famiglia, le famiglie)*

fantastic for *Fantastico (fantastico, fantastici, fantastica, fantastiche)*

far for *Lontano*

farm for *fattoria (la fattoria, le fattorie)*

farm holiday for Agriturismo (l'agriturismo, gli agriturismi)

fat for *Grasso (grasso, grassi, grassa, grasse)*

fate for *Fato (il fato)*

father for *Padre (il padre, i padri)*

father-in-law for *Suocero (il suocero, i suoceri)*

February for *Febbraio*

fee for *Tassa (la tassa, le tasse)*

feed oneself *(to) for Nutrirsi*

ferry for *Traghetto (il traghetto, i traghetti)*

fever for *Febbre (la febbre, le febbri)*

filling for *Piombatura (la piombatura, le piombature)*

fine for *Multa (la multa, le multe)*

finger for *Dito (il dito, le dita)*

finish *(to) for Finire*

fish for *Pesce (il pesce, i pesci)*

fish market for *Pescheria (la pescherie, le pescherie)*

fit *(to) for Andare bene*

fix *(to) for Riparare*

flavor for *Gusto (il gusto, i gusti)*

flight attendant for *Assistente di volo (l'assistente, gli assistenti)*

flip flops for *Infradito (l'infradito)*

flower for *Fiore (il fiore, i fiori)*

fly *(to) for Volare*

fog for *Nebbia (la nebbia)*

follow *(to) for Seguire*

foot for *Piede (il piede, i piedi)*

forget *(to)* for *Dimenticarsi*

formal for *formale*

foundation for *Fondotinta (il fondotinta, i fondotinta)*

fragrant for *Profumato (profumato, profumati, profumata, profumate)*

frame for *Montatura (la montatura, le montature)*

frequent for *Frequente*

frequently for *Frequentemente*

Friday for *Venerdì*

friend for *Amico (l'amico, gli amici, l'amica, le amiche)*

from for *Da*

frost for *Brina (la brina)*

fruit for *Frutta (la frutta, i frutti)*

gaiter for *Ghetta (la ghetta, le ghette)*

game for *Gioco (il gioco, i giochi)*

game for *Selvaggina (la selvaggina)*

gangway for *Passerella*

gas for *Benzina (la benzina, le benzine)*

gear for *Marcia (la marcia, le marce)*

generous for *Generoso (generoso, generosi, generosa, generose)*

get burned *(to)* for *Bruciarsi*

get dressed *(to)* for *Vestirsi*

get frightened *(to)* for *Spaventarsi*

get irritated *(to)* for *Irritarsi*

get ready *(to)* for *Prepararsi*

get sick *(to)* for *Ammalarsi*

get undressed *(to)* for *Svestirsi*

get up *(to) for Alzarsi*

get used to something *(to)* for *Abituarsi*

girl for *Ragazza (la ragazza, le ragazze)*

give *(to) for Dare*

glass for *Bicchiere (il bicchiere, i bicchieri)*

gloves for *Guanti (il guanto, i guanti)*

gluten for *Glutine*

gnocchi for *Gnocchi (lo gnocco, gli gnocchi)*

gnome for *Gnomo (lo gnomo, gli gnomi)*

go *(to)* for *Andare*

go down *(to) for Scendere*

goodbye *for Ciao*

go out *(to)* for *Uscire*

go up *(to)* for *Salire*

gondola for *Gondola (la gondola, le gondole)*

good for *Buono (buono, buoni, buona, buone)*

good, able for *Bravo (bravo, bravi, brava, brave)*

gram for *Grammo (il grammo, i grammi)*

granddaughter *for Nipote (la nipote, le nipoti)*

grandfather for *Nonno (il nonno, i nonni)*

grandmother for *Nonna (la nonna, le nonne)*

grandson for *Nipote (il nipote, i nipoti)*

grapefruit for *Pompelmo (il pompelmo, i pompelmi)*

grapes for *Uva (l'uva)*

gray for *Grigio (grigio, grigi, grigia, grigie)*

green beans for *Fagiolini (i fagiolini)*

green for *Verde*

greengrocer for *fruttivendolo (il fruttivendolo, i fruttivendoli)*

grocery store for *Negozio di alimentari (il negozio, i negozi)*

ground meat *for Macinata*

guest *for Ospite (l'ospite, gli ospiti)*

guitar for *Chitarra (la chitarra, le chitarre)*

gym for *Palestra (la palestra, le palestre)*

hail *(to)* for *Grandinare*

hair for *Capelli (i capelli)*

haircut for *Taglio di capelli*

ham for *Prociutto cotto (il prosciutto, i prosciutti)*

hand for *Mano (la mano, le mani)*

handsome *for Bello (bello, belli)*

happen *(to)* for *Accadere*

happily *for Felicemente*

happy for *Allegro (allegro, allegri, allegra, allegre)*

happy *for Felice (felice, felici)*

harbor for *Darsena (la darsena, le darsene)*

hat for *Cappello (il cappello, i cappelli)*

have *(to) for Avere*

have dinner *(to) for Cenare*

have fun *(to) for Divertirsi*

have lunch *(to) for Pranzare*

have to *(to) for Dovere*

haze for *Foschia*

he for *Lui*

head for *Testa (la testa, le teste)*

headset for *Cuffia (la cuffia, le cuffie)*

healed for *Guarito (guarito, guariti, guarita, guarite)*

hear *(to) for Sentire*

heavily *for forte*

hectogram for *Ettogrammo (ettogrammo, ettogrammi)*

heel *(of the foot) for Tallone (il tallone, i talloni)*

heel *(of the shoe)* for *Tacco (il tacco, i tacchi)*

hello *for Ciao*

hello for *Salve*

helm for *Timone (il timone, i timoni)*

help each other *(to)* for *Aiutarsi*

here for *Qui, qua*

highway *for Autostrada (l'autostrada, le autostrade)*

hindu for *Indù*

hoist *(to)* for *Issare*

holiday for *Festa (la festa, le feste)*

honest for *Onesto (onesto, onesti, onesta, oneste)*

honestly *for Onestamente*

honey for *Miele (il miele)*

hospital for *Ospedale (l'ospedale, gli ospedali)*

---

hostel for *Ostello (l'ostello, gli ostelli)*

hotel for *Albergo (l'albergo, gli alberghi)*

hotel owner for *Albergatore (l'albergatore, gli albergatori)*

house for *Casa (la casa, le case)*

hovercraft for *Overcraft*

how for *Come*

how much for *Quanto*

humid for *Umido (umido, umidi, umida, umide)*

husband for *Marito (il marito, i mariti)*

hydrofoil for *Aliscafo (l'aliscafo, gli aliscafi)*

hygiene for *Igiene (l'igiene)*

hypothesis for *Ipotesi (l'ipotesi, le ipotesi)*

I for *Io*

ice for *Ghiaccio (il ghiaccio)*

illusion for *Illusione (l'illusione, le illusioni)*

in front for *Davanti*

in front of for *Di fronte*

in for *In*

in order to for *Per*

included for *Incluso (incluso, inclusi, inclusa, incluse)*

independent for *Indipendente*

information desk for *Banco delle informazioni (il banco, i banchi)*

inside for *Dentro*

inspector for *Controllore (il controllore, i controllori)*

insurance for *Assicurazione (l'assicurazione, le assicurazioni)* *interest (to)* for Interessare

interest for Interesse (l'interesse, gli interessi)

interest rate for Tasso d'interesse

intersection for Incrocio (l'incrocio, gli incroci)

introduce oneself (to) for Presentarsi

island for Isola (l'isola, le isole)

jacket for Giacca (la giacca, le giacche)

jam for Marmellata (la marmellata, le marmellate)

January for Gennaio

jeans for Jeans (i jeans)

jewelry store for Gioielleria (la gioielleria, le gioiellerie)

joke for Scherzo (lo scherzo, gli scherzi)

July for Luglio

June for Giugno

keep (to) for Tenere

key for Chiave (la chiave, le chiavi)

kilogram for Chilogrammo (il chilogrammo, i chilogrammi)

kilometer for Chilometro (il chilometro, i chilometri)

kind for Gentile (gentile, gentili)

kindly for Gentilmente

kitchen for Cucina (la cucina, le cucine)

know each other (to) for Conoscersi

know (to) for Sapere

kosher for Kosher

lactose for Lattosio

land *(to) for Atterrare*

landing for *Atterraggio (l'atterraggio, gli atterraggi)*

last for *Ultimo (ultimo, ultimi, ultima, ultime)*

lastly *for Ultimamente*

late *(to be)* for *Essere in ritardo*

late for *Tardi*

later for *Più tardi*

laundromat for *Lavanderia (la lavanderia, le lavanderie) a gettoni or lavanderia automatica*

leave *(to) for Partire*

left *for Sinistra*

leg for *Gamba (la gamba, le gambe)*

lemon for *Limone (il limone, i limoni)*

lend *(to)* for *Prestare*

lens for *Lente (la lente, le lenti)*

lesson for *Lezione (la lezione, le lezioni)*

letter for *Lettera (la lettera, le lettere)*

lettuce for *Lattuga (la lattuga)*

liar for *Bugiardo (bugiardo, bugiardi, bugiarda, bugiarde)*

life belt for *Salvagente (il salvagente, i salvagente)*

lifeboat for *Scialuppa di salvataggio (la scialuppa, le scialuppe)*

life jacket for *Giubbotto di salvataggio* (il giubbotto, i giubbotti)

light blue for *Azzurro (azzurro, azzurri, azzurra, azzurre)*

light for *Leggero (leggero, leggeri, leggera, leggere)*

lightning for *Lampo (il lampo, i lampi)*

---

lightly *for Leggermente*

like *(to)* for *Piacere*

line for *Fila (la fila, le file)*

lipstick for *Rossetto (il rossetto, i rossetti)*

listen *(to)* for *Ascoltare*

liter for *Litro (il litro, i litri)*

live *(to)* for *Vivere, abitare*

living room for *Salotto (il salotto, i salotti)*

loafers for *Mocassini (i mocassini)*

loan for *Prestito (il prestito, i prestiti)*

lobster for *Aragosta (l'aragosta, le aragoste)*

long for *Lungo (lungo, lunghi, lunga, lunghe)*

look for *(to)* for *Cercare*

look *(to)* for *Guardare*

lose *(to)* for *Perdere*

lotion for *Crema (la crema, le creme)*

loudly *for forte*

love each other *(to)* for *Amarsi*

low calorie *for Ipocalorico*

low cholesterol *for Ipocolesterolemico or a basso contenuto di colesterolo*

low salt *for Iposodico*

lower *(to) for Calare*

luckily for *fortunatamente*

lucky for *fortunato (fortunato, fortunati, fortunata, fortunate)*

lunch for *Pranzo (il pranzo, i pranzi)*

mail for *posta (la posta)*

mailbox for *Cassetta delle lettere (la cassetta, le cassette)*

makeup for *Trucco (il trucco, i trucchi)*

man for *Uomo (l'uomo, gli uomini)*

March for *Marzo*

mascara for *Mascara (il mascara, i mascara)*

matter *(to)* for *Importare*

May for *Maggio*

meal for *Pasto (il pasto, i pasti)*

meat for *Carne (la carne, le carni)*

medium for *Medio (medio, medi, media, medie)*

meet with *(to)* for *Incontrarsi con*

melon for *Melone (il melone, i meloni)*

member for *Membro (il membro, i membri)*

menu for *Menù (il menù, i menù)*

messenger bag for *Borsa a tracolla (la borsa, le borse)*

meter for *Metro (il metro, i metri)*

metro for *Metropolitana (la metropolitana, le metropolitane)*

midnight for *Mezzanotte (la mezzanotte)*

mile for *Miglio (il miglio, le miglia)*

milk for *Latte (il latte)*

minimum for *Minimo (minimo, minimi, minima, minime)*

minute for *Minuto (il minuto, i minuti)*

mist for *Foschia*

monastery for *Monastero (il monastero, i monasteri)*

Monday *for Lunedì*

money order for *Vaglia postale*

money for *Soldi (il soldo, i soldi)*

month *for Mese (il mese, i mesi)*

monthly *for Mensile*

morning for *Mattina (la mattina, le mattine)*

morning for *Mattino (il mattino, i mattini)*

mother for *Madre (la madre, le madri)*

mother-in-law for *Suocera (la suocera, le suocere)*

motorboat for *Motoscafo (il motoscafo, i motoscafi)*

mountain for *Montagna (la montagna, le montagne)*

mouth for *Bocca (la bocca, le bocche)*

movie for *Film (il film, i film)*

Mr. and Mrs. *for Signori*

Mr. for *Signore*

Mrs. for *Signora*

much *for Molto*

much *(a lot) for Tanto*

museum for *Museo (il museo, i musei)*

mushroom for *Fungo (il fungo, i funghi)*

muslim for *Musulmano (musulmano, musulmani, musulmana, musulmane)*

nail polish for *Smalto (lo smalto, gli smalti)*

nap for *Pisolino (il pisolino, i pisolini)*

near *(close) for Vicino*

neck for *Collo (il collo, i colli)*

necklace for *Collana (la collana, le collane)*

need *(to) for Servire*

nephew for *Nipote (il nipote, i nipoti)*

never *for Mai*

new for *Nuovo (nuovo, nuovi, nuova, nuove)*

New Year for *Capodanno (il capodanno, i capodanni)*

newspaper for *Giornale (il giornale, i giornali)*

newsstand for *Giornalaio (il giornalaio, i giornalai)*

next for *Prossimo (prossimo, prossimi, prossima, prossime)*

next to for *Accanto*

nice for *Carino (carino, carini, carina, carine)*

niece for *Nipote (la nipote, le nipoti)*

night for *Notte (la notte, le notti)*

November *for Novembre*

now for *Adesso*

now *for Ora*

October for *Ottobre*

octopus for *Polipo (il polipo, i polipi)*

of *for Di*

offer *(to) for Offrire*

oil for *Olio (l'olio, gli olii)*

old for *Vecchio (vecchio, vecchi, vecchia, vecchie)*

olive/s for *Olive (l'oliva, le olive)*

on *(above) for Sopra*

onion for *Cipolla (la cipolla, le cipolle)*

open *(to)* for *Aprire*

opera for *Opera (l'opera, le opere)*

orange for *Arancia (l'arancia, le arance)*

orange for *Arancione*

orange tree *for Arancio (l'arancio, gli aranci)*

order *(to)* for *Ordinare*

gold for *Oro*

other, another *for Altro (altro, altri, altra, altre)*

otherwise for *Altrimenti*

outside for *Fuori*

over there *for Lì vicino*

overcast for *Nuvoloso*

owe *(to)* for *Dovere*

pacifier for *Ciuccio (il ciuccio, i ciucci)*

package for *Pacco (il pacco, i pacchi)*

painkiller for *Analgesico (l'analgesico, gli analgesici)*

painter for *Pittore (il pittore, i pittori)*

pair for *Paio (il paio, le paia)*

pancake for *Frittella (la frittella, le frittelle)*

panties for *Mutandina (la mutandina, le mutandine)*

passenger for *Passeggero (il passeggero, i passeggeri)*

passenger on foot for *Passeggero a piedi*

passport for *Passaporto*

pay (to) for *Pagare*

payee for *Beneficiario (il beneficiario, i beneficiari)*

payment for *Pagamento (il pagamento, i pagamenti)*

pea for *Pisello (il pisello, i piselli)*

peach for *Pesca (la pesca, le pesche)*

peach tree for *Pesco (il pesco, i peschi)*

pear for *Pera (la pera, le pere)*

pear tree for *Pero (il pero, i peri)*

pen for *Penna (la penna, le penne)*

pencil for *Matita (la matita, le matite)*

peninsula for *Penisola (la penisola, le penisole)*

percentage for *Percentuale (la percentuale, le percentuali)*

perfume store for *Profumeria (la profumeria, le profumerie)*

perm for *Permanente (la permanente, le permanenti)*

personal check for *Assegno personale (l'assegno, gli assegni)*

personal for *Personale*

pharmacy for *Farmacia (la farmacia, le farmacie)*

photo for *Foto (la foto, le foto)*

pigpen for *Porcile (il porcile, i porcili)*

pilgrim (female) for *Pellegrina (la pellegrina, le pellegrine)*

pilgrim (male) for *Pellegrino (il pellegrino, i pellegrini)*

pilot for *Pilota (il pilota, i piloti)*

pineapple for *Ananas (l'ananas, gli ananas)*

pink for *Rosa*

pizza for *Pizza (la pizza, le pizze)*

plastic for *Plastic (la plastica, le plastiche)*

platinum for *Platino*

platform for *Pensilina (la pensilina, le pensiline)*

play *(to)* for *Giocare*

pleasure *for Piacere*

plum for *Susina (la susina, le susine)*

pocket for *Tasca (la tasca, le tasche)*

point *(to) for Indicare*

police station for *Stazione di polizia (la stazione, le stazioni)*

pool for *Piscina (la piscina, le piscine)*

poor for *Povero (povero, poveri, povera, povere)*

pope for *Papa*

pork for *Maiale (il maiale, i maiali)*

port for *Babordo*

port for *Porto (il porto, i porti)*

postcard for *Cartolina (la cartolina, le cartoline)*

potato for *Patata (la patata, le patate)*

pour *(to)* for *Diluviare*

prawn or **shrimp** for *Gambero (il gambero, i gamberi)*

prayer for *Preghiera (la preghiera, le preghiere)*

price for *Prezzo (il prezzo, i prezzi)*

product for *Prodotto (il prodotto, i prodotti)*

professor *(female)* for *Professoressa (la professoressa, le professoresse)*

professor *(male)* for *Professore (il professore, i professori)*

---

program for Programma (il programma, i programmi)

prosciutto for Prociutto crudo (il prosciutto, i prosciutti)

psychologist for Psicologo (lo psicologo, gli psicologi)

pump for Pompa (la pompa, le pompe)

pumpkin for Zucca (la zucca, le zucche)

purchase for Acquisto (l'acquisto, gli acquisti)

purple for Viola

purse for Borsetta (la borsetta, le borsette)

put on makeup (to) for Truccarsi

put on (to) for Mettersi

queen for Regina (la regina, le regine)

quiet for Silenzioso (silenzioso, silenziosi, silenziosa, silenziose)

quiet for Zitto (zitto, zitti, zitta, zitte)

quietly for Silenziosamente

quietly for Piano

rabbit for Coniglio (il coniglio, i conigli, la coniglia, le coniglie)

radio for Radio (la radio, le radio)

raft for Zattera (la zattera, le zattere)

rain for Pioggia (la pioggia)

rain (to) for Piovere

rainbow for Arcobaleno (l'arcobaleno, gli arcobaleni)

raincoat for Impermeabile (l'impermeabile, gli impermeabili)

rarely for Raramente

read (to) for Leggere

receipt for Ricevuta (la ricevuta, le ricevute)

recent *for Recente*

red for *Rosso (rosso, rossi, rossa, rosse)*

refund *(to)* for *Rimborsare*

refund for *Rimborso (il rimborso, i rimborsi)*

register for *Cassa (la cassa, le casse)*

regret *(to)* for *Dispiacere*

rejoice *(to)* for *Rallegrarsi*

rent *(to)* for *Noleggiare*

rental car for *Macchina a noleggio (la macchina, le macchine)*

repair for *Riparazione (la riparazione, le riparazioni)*

repeat *(to) for Ripetere*

reserve *(to)* for *Prenotare*

rest *(to)* for *Riposare*

rest *(to)* for *Riposarsi*

restaurant for *Ristorante (il ristorante, i ristoranti)*

rested for *Riposato (riposato, riposati, riposata, riposate)*

return *(to)* for *Tornare*

rice dish for *Risotto (il risotto, i risotti)*

rich for *Ricco (ricco, ricchi, ricca, ricche)*

right *for Destra*

ring for *Anello (l'anello, gli anelli)*

river for *Fiume (il fiume, i fiumi)*

road for *Strada (la strada, le strade)*

room for *Stanza (la stanza, le stanze)*

rotary for *Rotatoria (la rotatoria, le rotatorie)*

rough for *Agitato (agitato, agitati, agitata, agitate)*

rowboat for *Barca a remi (la barca, le barche)*

rule for *Regola (la regola, le regole)*

sadly *for Tristemente*

sailboat for *Barca a vela (la barca, le barche)*

sail *(to)* for *Salpare*

sail for *Vela (la vela, le vele)*

sailor for *Marinaio (il marinaio, i marinai)*

salad for *Insalata (l'insalata, le insalate)*

salami for *Salame (il salame, i salami)*

salary for *Stipendio (lo stipendio, gli stipendi)*

sale for *Vendita*

salmon for *Salmone (il salmone, i salmoni)*

salt for *Sale (il sale, i sali)*

sandals for *Sandali (il sandalo, i sandali)*

sandwich for *Panino (il panino, i panini)*

Saturday *for Sabato*

save *(to)* for *Risparmiare*

say *(to) for Dire*

scarf for *Sciarpa (la sciarpa, le sciarpe)*

scene for *Scena (la scena, le scene)*

schedule *for Orario (l'orario, gli orari)*

school for *Scuola (la scuola, le scuole)*

sculptor for *Scultore (lo scultore, gli scultori)*

sculptress for *Scultrice (la scultrice, le scultrici)* *sea* for *Mare (il mare, i mari)*

seabass for *Branzino (il branzino, i branzini)*

season for *Stagione (la stagione, le stagioni)*

seat for *Posto (il posto, i posti)*

seat for *Sedile (il sedile, i sedili)*

seat-back for *Schienale (lo schienali, gli schienali)*

seatbelt for *Cintura di sicurezza (la cintura, le cinture)*

security for *Sicurezza*

see each other *(to) for Vedersi*

seem *(to)* for *Sembrare*

sell *(to)* for *Vendere*

September for *Settembre*

serve *(to)* for *Servire*

service station for *Stazione (la stazione, le stazioni) di servizio*

shake for *Scossa (la scossa, le scosse)*

share *(to)* for *Condividere*

shared for *Condiviso (condiviso, condivisi, condivisa, condivise)*

shawl for *Scialle (lo scialle, gli scialli)*

she for Lei

sheet for *Foglio (il foglio, i fogli)*

ship for *Nave (la nave, le navi)*

ship *(sailing)* for *Veliero*

shoe for *Scarpa (la scarpa, le scarpe)*

shock *(electric)* for *Scossa (la scossa, le scosse)*

shop assistant *(female)* for *Commessa (la commessa, le commesse) shopping mall* for *Centro commerciale (il centro commerciale, i centri commerciali)*

shopping (grocery) for *Spesa (la spesa)*

shopping for *Spese (le spese)*

short for *Corto (corto, corti, corta, corte)*

shorts for *Pantaloncini (i pantaloncini)*

shower for *Doccia (la doccia, le docce)*

shuttle for *Shuttle*

sick for *Malato (malato, malati, malata, malate)*

side dishes for *Contorni (il contorno, i contorni)*

signorina for *Signorina*

silly for *Sciocco (sciocco, sciocchi, sciocca, sciocche)*

silver for *Argento*

sincere for *Sincero (sincero, sinceri, sincera, sincere)*

single for *Singolo (singolo, singoli, singola, singole)*

sister for *Sorella (la sorella, le sorelle)*

sit (to) for *Sedersi*

size for *Taglia (la taglia, le taglie)*

ski for *Sci (gli sci)*

skirt for *Gonna (la gonna, le gonne)*

sky for *Cielo (il cielo)*

slap for *Schiaffo (lo schiaffo, gli schiaffi)*

sleep (to) for Dormire

slice for *Fetta (la fetta, le fette)*

slip for *Sottoveste (la sottoveste, le sottovesti)*

slippers for *Pantofole (la pantofola, le pantofole)*

slow for *Lento (lento, lenti, lenta, lente)*

slowly *for Lentamente, piano*

small hotel for *Pensione (la pensione, le pensioni)*

small for *Piccolo (piccolo, piccoli, piccola, piccole)*

smog for *Smog (lo smog, gli smog)*

snack for *Merenda (la merenda, le merende)*

sneakers for *Scarpe da ginnastica (la scarpa, le scarpe)*

snow *for Neve (la neve, le nevi)*

snow *(to) for Nevicare*

so and so *for Così così*

so long *for Arrivederci*

socks for *Calzini (il calzino, i calzini)*

softener for *Ammorbidente (l'ammorbidente, gli ammorbidenti)*

some *for Poco*

sometimes for *A volte*

son-in-law for *Genero (il genero, i generi)*

son for *Figlio (il figlio, i figli)*

song for *Canzone (la canzone, le canzoni)*

soon *for Presto*

soup for *Minestra (la minestra, le minestre)*

soup for *Zuppa (la zuppa, le zuppe)*

speak *(to)* for *Parlare*

spend *(to)* for *Spendere*

spice for *Spezia (la spezia, le spezie)*

spinach for *Spinaci (lo spinacio, gli spinaci)*

sport for *Sport (lo sport, gli sport)*

spring for *Primavera (la primavera, le primavere)*

square for *Piazza (la piazza, le piazze)*

stadium for *Stadio (lo stadio, gli stadi)*

star for *Stella (la stella, le stelle)*

starboard for *Tribordo*

station for *Stazione (la stazione, le stazioni)*

stationery store for *Cartoleria (la cartoleria, le cartolerie)*

stationery for *Carta da lettere (la carta, le carte)*

statue for *Statua (la statua, le statue)*

stay *(to) for Stare*

steak for *Bistecca (la bistecca, le bistecche)*

steamboat for *Vaporetto (il vaporetto, i vaporetti)*

still for *Fermo (fermo, fermi, ferma, ferme)*

stingy for *Avaro (avaro, avari, avara, avare)*

stomach for *Stomaco (lo stomaco, gli stomaci)*

store *(for clothing)* for *Negozio di abbigliamento (il negozio, i negozi)*

store for *Negozio (il negozio, i negozi)*

storm for *Burrasca (la burrasca, le burrasche)*

storm for *Temporale (il temporale, i temporali)*

straight *for Dritto*

strawberry for *Fragola (la fragola, le fragole)*

street for *Via (la via, le vie)*

---

suburban for *Interurbano*

sudden for *Improvviso*

suffer *(to) for Dolere*

sugar for *Zucchero (lo zucchero)*

suitcase for *Valigia (la valigia, le valige)*

summer *for Estate (l'estate, le estati)*

sun lotion for *Crema solare (la crema, le creme)*

sun for *Sole (il sole)*

Sunday for *Domenica*

supermarket for *Supermercato (il supermercato, i supermercati)*

surcharge for *Sovrapprezzo (il sovrapprezzo, i sovrapprezzi)*

sweater for *Maglione (il maglione, i maglioni)*

sweatshirt for *Felpa (la felpa, le felpe)*

sweet *for Dolce*

sweetly *for Dolcemente*

swim *(to)* for *Nuotare*

swordfish for *Pesce spada (il pesce spada, i pesce spada)*

system for *Sistema (il sistema, i sistemi)*

T-shirt for *Maglietta (la maglietta, le magliette)*

table for *Tavolo (il tavolo, i tavoli)*

take a bath *(to)* for *Farsi il bagno*

take advantage of *(to)* for *Approfittarsi (di)*

take off *(to)* for *Decollare*

take off for *Decollo (il decollo, i decolli)*

talk to each other *(to) for Parlarsi*

tar for *Catrame (il catrame)*

tasting for *Degustazione (la degustazione, le degustazioni)*

tea for *Tè (il tè, i tè)*

temperature for *Temperatura (la temperatura, le temperature)*

temporarily for *Provvisoriamente*

temporary for *Provvisorio*

thank you for Grazie

that for *Quello (quello, quelli, quella, quelle)*

theater for *Teatro (il teatro, i teatri)*

then for *Allora*

then for Poi

there for Lì, là

they for Loro, essi

thigh for *Coscia (la coscia, le cosce)*

thin for Magro (magro, magri, magra, magre)

thing for *Cosa (la cosa, le cose)*

this for *Questo (questo, questi, questa, queste)*

throat for *Gola (la gola, le gole)*

thunder for *Tuono (il tuono, i tuoni)*

Thursday for Giovedì

ticket booth, *office* for *Biglietteria (la biglietteria, le biglietterie)*

ticket for *Biglietto (il biglietto, i biglietti)*

tie for *Cravatta (la cravatta, le cravatte)*

tights for Collant (i collant)

time for *Tempo (il tempo, i tempi)*

tip for *Mancia (la mancia, le mance)*

tired for *Stanco (stanco, stanchi, stanca, stanche)*

tiring for *Stancante (stancante, stancanti)*

tissue, handkerchief for *Fazzoletto di carta (il fazzoletto, i fazzoletti)*

tobacco shop for *Tabaccheria (la tabaccheria, le tabaccherie)*

today for *Oggi*

toes for *Dita del piede*

toll for *Pedaggio (il pedaggio, i pedaggi)*

tomato for *Pomodoro (il pomodoro, i pomodori)*

tomorrow for *Domani*

too much for *Troppo*

tooth for *Dente (il dente, i denti)*

toothbrush for *Spazzolino da denti (lo spazzolino, gli spazzolini)*

tow truck for *Carro attrezzi (il carro attrezzi, i carri attrezzi)*

track for *Binario (il binario, i binari)*

traffic light for *Semaforo (il semaforo, i semafori)*

traffic policeman for *Vigile urbano*

train for *Treno (il treno, i treni)*

transfer *(to)* for *Trasferire*

transportation for *Trasporto (il trasporto, i trasporti)*

traveler's checks for *Travellers cheque*

traveler for *Viaggiatore (il viaggiatore, i viaggiatori)*

tray for *Vassoio (il vassoio, i vassoi)*

trip for *Gita (la gita, le gite)*

trousers for *Pantaloni (i pantaloni)*

trout for *Trota (la trota, le trote)*

trust *(to)* for *Fidarsi*

try on *(to) for Provare*

Tuesday *for Martedì*

tuna for *Tonno (il tonno, i tonni)*

turbulence for *Turbolenza (la turbolenza, le turbolenze)*

turkey for *Tacchino (il tacchino, i tacchini)*

turn *(to)* for *Girare*

turn off *(to)* for *Spegnere*

turn *(to)* for *Voltare*

turtle for *Tartaruga (la tartaruga, le tartarughe)*

U-turn for *Inversione a U*

ugly for *Brutto (brutto, brutti, brutta, brutte)*

umbrella for *Ombrello (l'ombrello, gli ombrelli)*

uncle for *Zio (lo zio, gli zii)*

under for *Sotto*

undershirt for *Canottiera (la canottiera, le canottiere)*

understand *(to) for Capire*

understand each other *(to) for Capirsi*

underwear for *Mutande (la mutanda, le mutande)*

until for *Fino*

until now *for Finora*

up here *for Quassù*

up there *for Lassù*

up there for *Lì sopra*

up there *(on top)* for *Lì in cima*

up for *Su*

urban for *Urbano*

usually for *Di solito*

validate *(to)* for *Obliterare*

valley for *Valle (la valle, le valli)*

vegan for *Vegano*

vegetable for *Verdura (la verdura, le verdure)*

vegetarian for *Vegetariano*

very much for *Assai*

villa for *Villa (la villa, le ville)*

village or **small town** for *Paese (il paese, i paesi)*

vinegar for *Aceto (l'aceto, gli aceti)*

vineyard for *Vigna (la vigna, le vigne)*

vomit *(to)* for *Vomitare*

wagon for *Carro (il carro, i carri)*

wait *(to)* for *Aspettare*

wake oneself up *(to)* for *Svegliarsi*

walk *(to)* for *Camminare*

want *(to)* for *Volere*

warm for *Caldo (caldo, caldi, calda, calde)*

washer for *Lavatrice (la lavatrice, le lavatrici)*

watch for *Orologio (l'orologio, gli orologi)*

watch seller for *Orologiaio (l'orologiaio, gli orologiai)* *watermelon* for *Anguria (l'anguria, le angurie)*

we for Noi

weak for *Debole (debole, deboli)*

weather for *Tempo (il tempo, i tempi)*

Wednesday for Mercoledì

week for *Settimana (la settimana, le settimane)*

weekly for *Settimanale*

welcome for *Benvenuto*

well for Bene

what for Cosa

what, which for Che

when for Quando

where for Dove

which for Quale

white for *Bianco (bianco, bianchi, bianca, bianche)*

who for Chi

why for Perché

wife for *Moglie (la moglie, le mogli)*

wind for *Vento (il vento, i venti)*

windbreaker for *Giubbotto* (il giubbotto, i giubbotti)

window for *Vetrina (la vetrina, le vetrine)*

window shopping (to) for *Guardare le vetrine*

wine dealer for Enoteca (l'enoteca, le enoteche)

wine for *Vino (il vino, i vini)*

winter for *Inverno (l'inverno, gli inverni)*

with *for Con*

withdrawal for *Prelievo (il prelievo, i prelievi)*

without *for Senza*

woman for *Donna (la donna, le donne)*

wonder *(to)* for *Domandarsi*

wonderful for *Meraviglioso (meraviglioso, meravigliosi, meravigliosa, meravigliose)*

work *(to)* for *Lavorare*

worry *(to) for Preoccuparsi*

wrist for *Polso (il polso, i polsi)*

write *(to) for Scrivere*

write to each other *(to) for Scriversi*

writer *(female)* for *Scrittrice (la scrittrice, le scrittrici)*

writer *(male)* for *Scrittore (lo scrittore, gli scrittori)*

year for *Anno (l'anno, gli anni)*

yellow for *Giallo (gialli, gialli, gialla, gialle)*

yesterday *for Ieri*

yogurt for *Yogurt (lo yogurt, gli yogurt)*

you *(many) for Voi*

you *for Tu*

you're welcome *for Prego*

young *for Giovane (giovane, giovani)*

zipper *for Cerniera lampo (la cerniera, le cerniere)*

zone *for Zone (la zona, le zone)*

Conclusion

Congratulations on making it through to the end of this book. It should have been informative and provided you with all of the tools you need to achieve your language learning goals.

Now, you can finally start the real journey, where you will apply your knowledge and express yourself more aptly and naturally and make your Italian shine. Plus, if you ever get stuck, you can always come back to this book at any time for a refresher lesson!

Finally, if you found this book useful in any way, a review on Amazon is always appreciated!

Check out another book by Simple Language Learning

.

Made in the USA
Las Vegas, NV
21 January 2022

41988116R00156